JOB INTERVIEWS

Where Both Can Win!

JOB INTERVIEWS

Where Both Can Win!

A no-nonsense guide for
Interviewees & Interviewers for the 21st century

Walter Vieira

UNICORN BOOKS

F-2/16, Ansari Road, Daryaganj, New Delhi-110002
☎ 23275434, 23262683, 23262783 • *Fax:* 011-23257790
E-mail: unicornbooks@vsnl.com • Website: www.unicornbooks.in

Distributors
Pustak Mahal®, Delhi
J-3/16, Daryaganj, New Delhi-110002
☎ 23276539, 23272783, 23272784 • Fax: 011-23260518
E-mail: info@pustakmahal.com • Website: www.pustakmahal.com

Sales Centres
- 10-B, Netaji Subhash Marg, Daryaganj, New Delhi-110002
  ☎ 23268292, 23268293, 23279900 • ***Fax:*** 011-23280567
  E-mail: salespmahal@airtelmail.in
  rapidexdelhi@indiatimes.com
- 6686, Khari Baoli, Delhi-110006
  ☎ 23944314, 23911979
- **Bengaluru:** ☎ 080-22234025 • ***Telefax:*** 080-22240209
  E-mail: pustak@airtelmail.in • pustak@sancharnet.in
- **Mumbai:** ☎ 022-22010941, 022-22053387
  E-mail: rapidex@bom5.vsnl.net.in
- **Patna:** ☎ 0612-3294193 • ***Telefax:*** 0612-2302719
  E-mail: rapidexptn@rediffmail.com
- **Hyderabad:** ***Telefax:*** 040-24737290
  E-mail: pustakmahalhyd@yahoo.co.in

ISBN 978-81-7806-157-3

Edition: 2009

Reprint: November 2010

Printed at : Param Offsetters, Okhla, New Delhi-110020

Preface

Are there not already many books on the art of interviewing and being interviewed, written by authorities in Europe and the United States, which have served the reading public all these years? What then, is the purpose of writing one more book on the same subject?

To the first question, I can only answer with a brief YES. The second question, however, needs some elaboration.

There are many books in the market that are directed at persons who will attend interviews (i.e. the Interviewees), but most of them are theoretical; and also too long. They are written in a style, which is too 'involved' for the people who need such a book most, that is, the young people in their teens and twenties. Probably the number of interviews one may have attended in the age group of 18-30 (12 years) and 30-60 (30 years) would be the same. But the experience of facing interviews in the latter age group would be qualitatively different, owing to the difference in maturity levels in the two age groups. People in the age group of 30-60 are generally more settled in life and hence more confident.

There are also many books on the market that are written for Interviewers. Many appear to be tomes written by personnel experts or psychologists, and therefore difficult to plough through after a busy working day. A book such as this can be 'run through' quickly covering most of the principles that the interviewer should know, or already knows but has forgotten.

Today there is a need for a readable book for those on either side of the table, i.e. both the interviewers and the interviewees. This book intends to fill that need, to build a bridge of communication, understanding, and appreciation for each other's situation. It will give readers an idea of what Interviewees and Interviewers need to do to perform well at the interview.

After all, the Interviewer and the Interviewee are not on opposite sides of the table (although physically they may be so). They are on the same side. The Interviewee wants a job where he/she will be happy. The

Interviewer wants a satisfied employee who will do the job well.

This book on Interviews will bring readers directly to their destination, without meandering through winding roads. It will guide the Interviewer on how to get the right person. It will show the Interviewee how to get the right job.

And when this happens it is a WIN-WIN situation for both.

It is 1 + 1 = 3.

– Walter Vieira

Acknowledgements

Though many of my ideas have been derived from the many books published on interviewing techniques, the major source of my learning has been through personal experiences gained through interactions with colleagues in the companies where I have worked as a corporate executive; from clients with whom I have had the privilege of working; and the hundreds of candidates I have interviewed in the past 40 years.

I must thank my secretary, Philomena Fonseca for having given special attention to doing up this manuscript and making suggestions for improving its presentation.

I also specially thank the following eminent managers in India, who have spared time to write their thoughts or relate anecdotes in spite of their very busy schedules. They have done this in a spirit of friendship and to extend support. Most important, they have done this as a contribution towards improving the quality of interviewing in the country. They are

1. Mr A K Agarwala, President, Hindalco Industries Limited
2. Mr Kalyan Banerjee, Ex Chairman, Exim Bank of India
3. Dr R Banerjee, Chairman, Lintas Limited *
4. Mr R Y Gaitonde, Chairman, The Gaitonde Group *
5. Dr Vinayshil Gautam, Professor, IIT Delhi
6. Mr Jamshed J Irani, Managing Director, Tata Steel
7. Mr B H Kothari, Chairman, H C Kothari Group of Companies
8. Mr Habil Khorakiwala, Chairman, Wockhardt Limited
9. Mr V G Rajadhyaksha, Ex Chairman, Hindustan Lever *
10. Dr P N Singh, Ex-President, Bombay Management Association

* deceased

Contents

Section-I (Focus on Interviewer)

Section-II (Focus on Interviewee)

Section-III (Focus on Interviewer / viewee)

Chapter 1

The Challenge of Interviews: What Do Companies Want in the 21st Century?

"Challenges are Motivators in Disguise"

Required – World Class Attitudes

Most companies all over the world now exist in an environment where survival depends on employing people who will do whatever it takes to:

- keep costs down
- keep quality high, and
- continuously look for new ways to add value to the customer.

Jackie Freiberg, author of *NUTS*, says that 'this requires more than compliance or meeting the educational qualifications. It requires people who are committed to taking personal responsibility for offering sensational service. It requires people who are willing to think and act as owners. These are people with the 'right attitudes'.

I have seen large consignments of textiles from Asia rejected by a buyer in USA because of pigeon droppings on a few rolls. It reflected negligence and 'poor attitude' of workers and supervisors on the night shift at a textile mill ten thousand miles away!

An aircraft pilot's lousy attitude spills over to the flight crew; who in turn, pass this on to the customers.

The restaurant manager's hostile attitude is reflected in the chef's poor offering and the waiter's grudging service.

The company's hiring patterns will determine its culture, service standards, reputation and as a consequence, turnover and profit.

What a new recruit 'knows' can be changed and improved, but what a new recruit 'is', is less likely to change as fast.

Freiberg gives four keys to hiring the best:

- Identify the people in your own organisation who already have the kind of attributes you want. After checking with customers, peers, subordinates and superiors, build an attitudinal profile and use this to hire new people.
- Design clever, creative recruiting ads to entice the right people to apply. These ads should be unconventional and will be successful in attracting people with the right attitudes.
- Screen candidates for attitudes like unselfishness, flexibility, fun, initiative or a propensity to take risks. "Can you tell me about a time when you broke rules to meet a customer's need?" "Can you tell me how you used humour to diffuse a tense situation?"
- Draw applicants back to specific examples of how they have demonstrated the attitudes you want. Focus more on what they have done in the past rather than vague promises of what they will do for you when they join you.

Leaders in industry today, set the tone for success by screening and hiring world-class people with world-class attitudes.

It is getting the right person; and matching her/him with the right job. In a highly competitive world, where customer is the king, the interviewer and interviewee are on the same side of the table with one objective – to create and keep a customer.

Corporate Mission – Seeking Alignment

The Corporate Mission is the benchmark against which all hiring/ selection decisions are to be taken. The question to be asked is "Is this hiring decision complying with our mission statement?"

(a) This mission should always be kept in mind by all people hiring personnel, irrespective of the department or function.

(b) This mission should be reviewed every 3/5 years, as the company's requirements will change from time to time in accordance with internal and external changes.

It is therefore essential that interviewees are familiar with the mission of a company before the interview; so that they can check whether their own goals match the company's goals.

This simple precaution can save a lot of heartburn and regrets later – both for the company and for the individual.

An aside

Raj, an ineffective salesman, was talking about how he got started in sales: "I started out on the theory that the selling world had an opening for me and it certainly did. I am in that hole now."

Chapter 2

The High Cost of Hiring the Wrong Person

"A stitch in time, saves nine"

This is the attention getting caption headline of an advertisement of a hiring company called *Hire the Best*, in Virginia, USA.

Although an advertisement, the body copy makes interesting reading and makes the following points:

Some people go to great lengths to ensure they hire the right person. For instance, when Bob, the owner of a San Diego-based company, narrows his search down to two or three candidates, he invites each one to dinner. But the candidate is unaware that the restaurant belongs to Bob's friend and the waiter is instructed to screw up their order.

If he orders a steak *well-done*, he gets it *rare*, and Bob watches his reaction. If he complains to the waiter, Bob knows he's an assertor (a lot of drive, but may prove to be *too pushy*).

But if he says nothing, Bob asks, *"How's your food"*? If he replies with, *"Fine,"* it reveals that he's a realtor (eager to get along, and may be too accommodating and a *pushover*).

To be certain, Bob says, *"I thought you ordered well-done."* If he answers, *"I did, and normally I'd mention it to the waiter, but I'm here because of the job, not because of the food,"* he reveals himself to be a discerner (good at setting priorities, quick at sorting the important from the superfluous, and knows how to act appropriately in each situation). Bob has found who he's looking for.

Bill Gates is even tougher. Job applicants can have a great resume, excellent references, perfect job experience and present themselves well in an interview, but Gates bases his decision on the moment when he casually asks.*"How much artificial turf is in North America?"* or *"Why are manhole covers round?"* The next thing the candidate says determines if he or she gets the job. Gates doesn't expect, or want, the right answer. He's interested in their *thinking process.*

The stakes are high when you're recruiting. The industry rule of thumb is: the *wrong person* costs you *three times* their annual salary. A $50,000 employee costs you $1,50,000; a $150,000 employee costs $450,000. That's for starters. There's also lost opportunity cost... plus lost business, potential customers, and momentum. And you're back to square one, looking for a replacement.

It can even become a nightmare, as one man learned: "When I hired Frank, my wife asked me, 'How well do you know him?' Eight months later I spent $1.4 million and one month in court with Frank. I'll never forget that question."

How well do you know the person you're hiring? In this article, you will discover a remarkably foolproof way – used by America's fastest growing and most successful companies – to *find, hire* and *keep the best employees.*

Twenty years ago, a man by the name of Ed Ryan, developed a remarkably simple method that determines – with uncanny accuracy which person to hire. The results are so impressive, that hundreds of companies gladly pay for Ryan's team to screen candidates to fill *one opening.*

"It does sound expensive," says Jeri Christopher, Vice President of Human Resources at Gordon Bailey & Associates in Atlanta. *"But it saves us tens of thousands of dollars in two ways: First, it saves time. Ed's screening process speeds things up because we can rule out a lot of candidates quickly over the phone. And second, once we hire, the position is usually filled for a long time."*

Ed Ryan discovered that most companies have difficulty in finding top people because of three common mistakes.

First, they hire someone for what they *know*, and then fire them for who they *are.*

Second, they hire quickly and fire slowly. That's backwards, according to Ryan.

Third, and the biggest reason why companies get stuck with the wrong people is, that they base their hiring decision on a person's previous experience.

"Deadly Mistake!" says Ryan. "Previous experience is a poor indicator of a person's future performance. The best is to look at their behavioural traits – who they are as a person, what drives them, how they make decisions, how they work and interact with others."

"For instance, at EDS, when Ross Perot was looking for department managers, he hired teachers because they could manage, even though they knew nothing about data systems. Gates and Perot know that people can learn information and skills; they can't learn behavioural traits. People with the right traits will learn surprisingly quickly. Not everyone has what it takes to be a good manager. It requires traits that have nothing to do with expertise in an area. Find a person with these natural traits and you've found a good manager.

"And the same holds true if you're looking for salespeople, engineers, CEOs, financial people, researchers, fundraisers, receptionists, secretaries, drivers, nurses... or any job position you can think of... and in any industry. Each job has its own set of traits required to do well and be the best."

Ryan developed a simple method that lets people *read anyone like a book* – without the other person ever knowing it – simply by asking a set of ordinary questions. *"By asking 'loaded' questions,"* he says, *"You don't have to be a mind reader. When people answer, they automatically reveal themselves to you – and they don't even realise that they're divulging private information. Even if they try to hide their weak points, they'll surface – every time. Everything that you need to know is suddenly out in the open. No more relying on gut feel. And there are fewer surprises later."*

Ryan has identified the 25 *behavioural traits* that accurately *predict* how a person will perform on the job. These traits have nothing to do with intelligence, knowledge, experience, personality or education. But, they have everything to do with *how they are as people*, how they instinctively *do things*, and how they *make decisions* from moment to moment. The 25 traits fall into 4 categories.

1. Motivation : *what drives a person.* Some jobs require people who are motivated by ego, others by ideals or by what's best for the group.

2. Think : *how a person gathers information and reaches a decision.* One job requires people who are slow and thorough; another needs those who prefer to make split-second decisions on minimal information.

3. Act : *how a person does their job.* One job requires people who work best alone; while other jobs need those who work best in a group. Some jobs attract people who love variety; other jobs need those who prefer routine.

4. Interact : *how a person interacts with others.* Some jobs need people who are confrontational; another job needs someone who is accommodating.

There are no rights or wrongs in behavioural traits, just *natural preferences* – much like a preference for using your right or left hand.

"*But here's the interesting part,*" says Ryan. "*When we examined the top 10 salespeople in the country, we found that 9 of them share the same traits. And it's the same in every job – regardless if it's a CEO, secretary, nurse, valet, researcher, department head, teacher, engineer or truck driver. 9 out of the top 10 in that specific job score high in the same set of traits. Out of the 25 possible traits, each job has its own set of 5-7 key traits that stand out as being critical. We call this set of traits, the "Top Performer Profile."*"

The "*Top Performer Profile*" is the *benchmark* – your yardstick or shopping list – by which you measure each candidate. When you find a person whose built-in traits for motivation, thinking, acting and interaction match those required by a specific job, you've found someone who will fit the job, and your organisation, like a glove.

To find this person, you start with the required set of critical traits – the *Top Performer Profile* – and then ask the candidate a series of questions designed to measure how close he comes to matching the profile. Each job is unique, so each *Top Performer Profile* has its own set of questions.

The *Top Performer Profile* simplifies your search and evaluation and gives you the upper hand in an interview. And it saves you time too. During your first phone conversation, several quick questions will reveal if the candidate has the required traits. In just a few moments, you'll know if a person is worth investing more time and resources in.

One of the beauties of *Hiring the Best* is that you don't even have to know anything about the job you're filling. Until now, only a top performer could spot another top performer in the same category. For example; a good salesman can spot another good salesman, a good engineer can easily pick out another good engineer, etc. But with *Hiring the Best*, you don't have to understand computers to find a top computer engineer. The same applies to finance, medicine, marketing, welding or any job.

With your *Top Performer Profile* as your guide, ask Ryan's series of questions and you'll know if the person's inner motivation, decision-making style, preferred work pattern and the way they interact matches other top performers. "Either they match what you're looking for, or they don't. If they don't," Ryan says, "don't hire them." He adds, "*The reason why so few companies succeed in building a true Dream Team is this: it's been said that talent goes downhill. By that I mean, if you're a ten, you'll hire a nine. The nine who's working for you will hire an eight. The eight hires a seven and down it goes. Inferior people work for superior people. But, for any company to grow, it must be full of tens – people who are the BEST at what they do in their area of expertise.*

A Real Situation

This can also happen. Sam was hired as Marketing Manager for India for a UK based pharmaceutical company, by the International Division Director in UK. At the same time the company hired Roy as Marketing Director to whom the Marketing Manager would report.

Sam did not mind this, except that Roy was 6, when Sam was 9. Over a period of time, Roy was jealous, envious and finally vindictive; all arising from a basic sense of insecurity and fear. He made life difficult for Sam. Minor issues became major problems. Sam finally left the organisation and became a successful entrepreneur.

All is well that ends well!

Kathleen Douglass, President of Greensheet Corp, in Houston says, "*I am impressed with being able to match people to the responsibilities and expectations; and then finding people who will successfully perform and work in our specific environment.*"

And Chris Shoemaker, HR Director for Frankel & Co. in Chicago said, "*It has de-mystified and simplified the hiring process.*"

Chapter 3

What Kind of Work Would You Like to do?

"If you really love what you do,
You will not have to work a day in your life"

The first question to honestly ask yourself when looking for a job after high school or college, or when looking for a change in job is – What kind of work would you like to do?

The world is full of people who are doing a job because they ambled into it or because they have no other choice.

What would you like to do?

There are those who have no will to make a break from the existing situation; who have been forced into a job or have been attracted by the money it brings. Others follow their father's profession when they have no inclination or love for it. Still others have followed the herd instinct and become part of the herd.

Like the three wise men in the Bible, who followed a star and covered hundreds of miles on camel-back, each person must set a goal, some objective, and follow it. That is the most important thing – to have an aim in life; to want to do something, which you really like, no matter what it is.

You can be an artist, an interior decorator, an automobile mechanic, an electronics engineer, a neurosurgeon or a laboratory technician. If you really like what you do, you will enjoy it; and what's more, you will become very good at it. It is much better to be a first class motor mechanic than a third-rate doctor.

A Real Situation

My friend Carl became a medical practitioner because his father was a doctor. Unfortunately, he could not get into medical school on merit. So his father 'bought' a seat for him at one of the private colleges in the South. Carl took eight years to finish the five-year programme. He then came back to Mumbai and practised at his father's clinic. His practice never picked up. After a struggle for ten years, Carl took to drink. His small practice further declined. Now Carl's son has also gone to medical school – because the medical profession is a family tradition! It has now gone into the third generation, and another disinterested, average general practitioner will be born!

And if you are capable and lucky, then perhaps both money and fame will follow. It may not be on a national level but certainly you will be respected in your community, in your city or perhaps in your small town. And more important, you will respect yourself. The internal mental conflicts and emotional stress will be minimal. Your attitude will be right and your customers, your superiors, and your company will be happy with you. You will be a contributor, and you will have job satisfaction. Life will be worth living.

A Real Situation

It was Larry Noronha who taught me the truth of the old adage that "a man's grasp should match his reach".

Larry Noronha was a very successful salesman. He was the seniormost salesman of the company in 1952 and had been working in the Mumbai city area for 14 years. All this time the company kept growing. With an increase in the number of salesmen, Mr Tellis, the Managing Director, felt the need for a sales manager to guide and control this increased number. Life was simpler in the 1950s and the director envisaged a simple organisation structure of just 30 salesmen reporting to a sales manager.

He asked Larry Noronha to take over this new position. Larry was his seniormost salesman, and was both effective and popular. He was also an actor in amateur theatre and therefore well-known in circles beyond the limited business world.

Much to Mr Tellis' surprise, Larry turned down the offer. He enjoyed being a salesman. He liked the freedom of the salesman's job and the way his customers showed confidence in him. He didn't want to 'be responsible for a group of other people.' He felt that his own capability and temperament would not allow him to be a successful sales manager. With permission, he suggested the name of a junior colleague who was then selected.

When the field force was further expanded four years later, there was a need for a deputy sales manager and Larry was offered this assignment. Again, he turned it down with the same self-evaluation.

Not many people can say 'No' to a promotion with more money and better status. But Larry knew how far his reach matched his grasp. This is a quality few people have mastered. Larry died prematurely of cancer–a professional salesman, loved and respected by his colleagues, his customers and a large number of his theatre fans.

So every young person must choose a road. As the Chinese saying goes; "If you don't know where you are going, then all roads will lead you nowhere."

Chapter 4

What Kind of Work Can You Do?

"Identify your talents. You are the sum total of all your choices up until this moment"

You have to be realistic about the kind of work you can do. You may like to be a screen actor but your talents may not lie there. You may like to be an engineer, but may be poor at mathematics; or you may like to be a lawyer, but have a poor memory and a poor command of language.

It is therefore necessary for every individual to do what, in management science, is called a SWOT analysis. SWOT is not a complicated theory. In fact, it is very simple. It is a measurement of S-strengths and W-weaknesses; of O-opportunities and T-threats. It requires an honest look at yourself, at your capabilities and incapabilities; at what can be achieved if you honestly try hard and what cannot be achieved at all. It also requires a clear assessment of all the threats and dangers and opportunities that may be present in the field you choose.

Obviously, if you are weak in mathematics and very strong in languages, you have to think about areas, which involve qualitative faculties. Perhaps you can become a lawyer, writer, journalist, author, solicitor, or a professor in languages. If you are strong in mathematics you can become an engineer, physicist, or astronomer.

Some people are prima donnas who like to work and achieve alone and they should focus on a profession, which is individualistic. Some people are gregarious and like to work with other people and be with people, most of the time. They would be qualified to be members or leaders of teams involved in group working.

Be realistic about what you can do

> ## A Real Situation
>
> **Diverse Interests**
>
> I first met Alex in Paris. His family is from Mauritius and he was doing a Masters in Physics and Maths at the Sorbonne University. A few years later, I heard that Alex had gone to the US to do a PhD in petroleum technology. I met him again a few years later, in the UK where he was finishing a degree in law at Cambridge. After this he went back to Mauritius and began what is now a flourishing law practice.
>
> Alex is an unusual person. He has many talents. Most of us do not encompass such a range. There are many things he could do – and he finally chose one of them, law. The question still arises – did Alex waste time doing physics and petroleum technology? Or can it be explained always as a training of the mind?

Some people are doers and, therefore may like an 'activity-oriented' profession. Some are thinkers and planners and are inclined to be desk-bound in departments like 'corporate planning'. A few are what are called 'integrators' – a balance of thinking and doing people. This is that rare breed who can generally reach the top, because they combine both faculties and are very strong, both at conceptual thinking as well as implementation of their plans.

An aside

"This job has no great future" I said. "It is only a junior Accounts clerk assignment."

"That's alright, Mr Vieira" he answered "I would like to take it. I don't want to go very far or anywhere" he replied.

Chapter 5

Looking for The Right Opportunities

"Look at every obstacle as an opportunity"

There are many ways of looking for the right opportunities.

The most obvious one is to look at the advertisements in the Appointment pages, or Vacancies columns in the newspapers or business magazines. Then send your biodata to the relevant companies if your profile matches their requirements.

If you are fresh out of school or university then you need not be overly cautious when responding to these advertisements. You can respond even to an advertisement given under a Box Number where the name of the company is not disclosed.

But if you are already employed, and are not looking seriously for a change in assignment, but merely shopping around, then it is not prudent to respond to advertisements that come with just a Box Number. You may be writing to your own company or perhaps, even to your own boss. It is always safer to know which company you are applying to.

You could perhaps spot opportunities through friends and acquaintances. They may tell you about a vacancy which has arisen in the organisation where they are working, or about a new project or some expansion where perhaps your talents and background could fit very well.

Another source of opportunities is employment agencies or selection consultants. You may like to keep your biodata in their data bank. If any opportunity does arise which matches your profile, they will get in touch with you. Care should be taken to pick just one or two good agencies, which are also appropriate to your kind of occupation. (There are some age ncies which specialise in sales personnel, others in accounts personnel, etc). If a company that asks for recommendations finds that your biodata is sent by four recruiting agencies, they will get the impression that you are registered everywhere and therefore are at a 'loose end' or desperately looking for an assignment. Your market value goes down immediately and substantially.

The agency is always expected to disclose the name of the company to you before it discloses your name to the company. If this is not the agency's practice, you can stipulate that your biodata should not be sent to clients, unless you agree to them doing so.

However, never ignore head-hunters or be curt with them. You never know when you will need them, in the future.

Look out for the right opportunities

Sometimes you could make a direct approach because an assignment or industry appeals to you and interests you. You could be an observer of the general economic scene and then decide to apply to a bank because you would like to work in that kind of enterprise. Perhaps you may like to begin in the Curators office at the National Museum or work in the office of the National Centre for Performing Arts. It is possible that there may or may not be an existing vacancy. Perhaps seeing your interest and enthusiasm, they will create a vacancy because they see a person with both ability and keenness to join them.

You could perhaps apply on a speculative basis and write to companies, which you think may have a vacancy. Some candidates telephone Personnel Managers and go and meet them with the biodata and take a chance. Sometimes these people succeed. Other times a move like this may irritate company executives who may say that they have no time, or that a vacancy does not exist. This is a chance you have to take.

Now, there are opportunities on the Net. Companies in India like Naukri.com, Monster.com, solicit CVs to be included in their data bank. This service is free. Then recruiters reach out to this bank with their specifications and try and find a match. Because of the convenience and capacity of the net, thousands of CVs can be classified, and yet the right match can easily be accessed in a very short time. The market place has changed to the market space!

A Real Situation

Swamy was working at the Mumbai Airport as a Traffic Assistant. One day a friend approached him to say that his International Company Chairman was arriving. Could Swamy somehow manage to get the local Managing Director to receive and welcome the Chairman 'inside' the 'no visitors allowed' area? Pulling the right strings, Swamy managed to do this. The Managing Director was very appreciative. When the group was leaving the airport, the Managing Director, Whitby, told Swamy that he was welcome to come see him anytime at the office, if Swamy needed anything. A week later, Swamy did phone Mr. Whitby and fixed an appointment. He told Whitby that he was fed up of the Traffic Assistant job, which was also a dead-end assignment. Was there anything that he could do with his pass class B.A. degree, in this large toiletries conglomerate? Swamy was hired as Regional Sales Manager for Western India. Whitby felt that with his people skills and his gift of the gab, Swamy would perform - and Swamy did perform. He rose to be General Manager of a Division before he left the company to become General Manager of another company. Had Swamy ignored the invitation to see Whitby and considered Whitby's invitation merely a 'social nicety' - Swamy would have perhaps still been a senior Traffic Assistant fifteen years later!

If you are in a university or other tertiary institution, the best thing to happen would be to be selected by a company at campus interviews where you virtually breeze into the company. It is the company that comes to you, rather than you going to the company.

However, the vast majority of young people (and the not so young) will have to search for and identify the right opportunities by themselves using one of the five approaches mentioned earlier.

In finding job opportunities we need to use the same basic and classical methods that we may use in prospecting in marketing –

- keep your eyes and ears open (to pick up any nuggets of information)
- use the endless chain method (one recruiter referring to another; one friend referring to another
- the centre of influence method (using a central point who has many contacts, e.g. recruitment agency; recruitment consultant).

An aside

A plant had just hired a new employee, a man in his early twenties. On the first day of work, he arrived 45 minutes late.

"What happened?" asked the foreman.

The young man replied quite seriously, "I had been looking for work for so long, I forgot I had a job!"

Chapter 6

The Curriculum Vitae (CV)

"People know you by what you tell them about yourself"

Once you have decided where you are going to apply for a job, the next step is to draft the application. You must ensure that your application stands out from the crowd – and gets noticed. It takes time and effort, to master the art of making your application "different," to be distinguishable, and to be set apart. In fact, it takes so much time and effort, that in the USA, where specialisation is carried to the extreme, there are "application specialists" who prepare applications for clients, at a fee.

Positive Aspects – What To Do

Use good quality white bond paper to type the application and use matching quality and colour envelope. If you have personal stationery, even if it is coloured, but not garish, this is acceptable. Have an envelope larger than the contents.

Get the application neatly typed, with a layout pleasing to the eye, and without errors. Sometimes applications addressed to me have my name spelled wrongly. They address it to Valtar Wera! How can an employer call a candidate to an interview, when the latter displays such obvious carelessness?

Use a brief covering letter of not more than one page to your CV (curriculum vitae or biodata) which highlights your qualifications and experience, which are especially relevant to the job, you are applying for. It helps to focus on how your skills match with what the employer is looking for, based on his advertisement. It also shows that you have read the Ad carefully and given thought to the employer's needs and the contribution you can make. It demonstrates that you are not just looking for 'any' job!

It is also important that all the strengths are properly highlighted, especially the strengths, which would have a bearing on the job; and that the weaknesses are de-emphasised but not totally eliminated or cursorily glossed over. To the interviewer this will reflect on the honesty of the candidate and therefore make him or her more receptive.

Applications must be addressed properly, dated and have a complete address. If the application is not addressed to a Manager in a specific department, e.g. Sales Manager, Electronics Division; then it should be addressed to the Personnel Manager. But it should never be sent to just "M/s Zeeman's Ltd." It will then probably be dealt with by the Receptionist! Even worse is to address it 'to whom it may concern'! This will never get to the 'target within the company.'

You must give all the details including the name of your present employer. Some applicants keep this name a closely guarded secret. I have never been able to find the reason for such secrecy. It serves no purpose.

It is a good practice to give the names of two references in the biodata. However, the references should be known to you; not just known to your uncle. The references should also be appropriate to the level of the job applied for. It does seem ridiculous to apply for a job as Accounts Assistant, and to have references of the Commander in Chief of the Indian Army or the Governor of a State. Your college professor or former boss, someone who knows you well enough, and has some evidence of your performance and ability, are always better referees to use.

Please always obtain prior permission from the referees and only then give their names as References.

Later, do keep them informed whether you did or did not get the assignment. These are basic courtesies.

It is also necessary to clarify if you are agreeable to be located anywhere in the country, or whether the choices are restricted to a few, or even one location. Some candidates imply that they are prepared to be posted anywhere but when it comes to the final stage, they insist that they can accept a posting only in Mumbai, or Bangalore or wherever, which can cause a lot of annoyance to the employer.

And what emoluments do you expect? Some write vaguely, that their present emoluments are Rs 250,000 annually, plus the 'usual' perks. What are the 'usual' perks? Is it a house, car, and chauffeur? It could mean anything or yet nothing. Once again, instead of helping you, such camouflaging of the actual emoluments, is an approach, which will only project an image of a person who does not clearly give all the facts.

The bio data attached to the covering letter should be complete in all respects and should have the right sequence, as follows:

1. Name in full
2. Address
   Telephone Number
3. Date of Birth
4. Marital Status
5. Languages (Spoken)
   (Read)
   (Written)
6. Educational Qualifications
7. Special Assignments
   (Details of Thesis, Project Work, etc.)
   (Any prizes, awards)
8. Short Courses done with the period mentioned
9. Professional Membership
10. Employment history
    (in chronological order, present employment first)
11. Briefly state responsibilities and achievements in present job.
12. Significant contributions made.
13. Hobbies and Extra Curricular Activities
14. References (at least two)
15. Salary Expected**
16. If selected, date of joining

** I suggest you mention "Negotiable" stating the figure.

An example of Previous Experience and Career Objectives is given in the box below:

> Bio-data of:
>
> Mr Suresh Borkar, ACA, MBA
>
> Hampton Court, Central Avenue
>
> Santacruz West, Mumbai 400054
>
> Tel: 523568
>
> Previous Experience: Summary
>
> Started my career as a corporate analyst in the headquarters of a divisionalised Public Company in Mumbai.
>
> Had in-depth training in implementation and administration of Management Planning and Control Systems, financial and operational monitoring, scrutiny and evaluation of capital expenditure proposals.
>
> In the second assignment, was responsible as Management Accountant for design and implementation and subsequent administration of an integrated accounting system, review and streamlining of support systems for effective budgetary control, long range planning, cost reduction and profit monitoring and treasury, financial and management accounting, corporate taxation, budgetary control and day-to-day running of a large department.
>
> In the third assignment in Singapore, was jointly responsible with the directors for organising the launch of a furniture business. On a routine basis was responsible for all commercial, financial and statutory aspects of the business.
>
> In the current assignment, as financial controller, besides routine responsibilities of budgetary control, accounting and finance, am also responsible for corporate taxation, systems and procedures, corporate internal audit and data processing.
>
> Career Objectives
>
> I am a self-starter, with skills of exercising an 'executive view', and decision making ability to deal with operating details. I wish to reach the topmost echelons of a professional organisation, which offers ample opportunities for organisational and individual growth.

What To Avoid

A job application should not be handwritten, especially if your handwriting is not easily decipherable, unless the advertisement specifically says so. It is best to restrict handwriting to just the signature, and have the rest of the matter typed.

A job application should not be an 'obvious' photocopy of an original. This shows that you have been sending applications all over the place, and this is one of the many. You may actually be sending applications all over, and there is nothing wrong with that, but this does not mean that you should 'project' such an image.

Illegible handwritten applications, photocopies, cyclostyled sheets and faint typed copies will all end up in the waste paper basket, while you wait and hope for an interview call letter.

Do not use your company's letterhead and envelope to write your application. This is not acceptable. Using company stationery for personal work, and perhaps even using company postage is a reflection of a certain laxity in personal integrity. It is not the quantum of money but the principle involved.

Do not be careless or generous with the amount of gum used on the envelope, otherwise some part of the application would get stuck and the application would get torn in the process of opening the envelope. Very few in the unfamiliar employer's firm will take the trouble to join pieces together. And so, whatever is torn off is missed, and with that, a part of why you should be selected for the assignment.

If you are blessed with a large number of well-placed relatives, you must not plug this fact hard in the biodata. If you give details of the qualifications and position held by father, brother, sister and in-laws, the employer may be more impressed with the achievements of the relatives, rather than perhaps, your own achievements!

Don't Act 'Smart'

It is most important to ensure that the biodata is complete in all respects – that all the information is included, and that it is in the proper sequence. In our experience there have been many situations where candidates have not followed basic rules.

Once there was an application where the candidate had given all the details, except his name. The company could not even get in touch

Your CV, or biodata, must tell enough but it must also be kept brief

with him! There are those who try to hide some facts, like not disclosing their age because they do not fit into the age requirement that has been specified. Or, they mention the age only at the end of the biodata, thus distorting the normal sequence.

A Real Situation

Incomplete Information

Dr Roy came to me through a friend. I was told that Dr Roy was in India on a short holiday; that he had done a doctorate from the USA; and that he worked for a large corporation in Cyprus, in the area of strategic planning. He was investigating the possibility of taking up an assignment in India, if he could find something suitable.

I had in mind a position with a client of mine. So I had an extended chat with Roy. Something in the well written and well laid out CV, seemed odd. And then I honed in on the fact that Roy had finished his Ph.D. in just one and a half years, and when he was still working. How could that be?

Roy then admitted that he had done the Ph.D. by correspondence. What he did not elaborate was that it was from a university where a Ph.D. is granted virtually on payment of a fee!

Finally the application must not be a hard selling effort. It must be a soft sell, making the customer 'want to buy'. It must follow all the basic rules of effective communication. While it 'tells enough', it must also be brief, using the right tone (neither servile nor hostile) to show how the employer will benefit from the services you have to offer.

A Real Situation : Screening the CVs

It was a herbal medicine manufacturing company in India – a large one and in existence for 80 years. The Chairman had asked me to recruit a Marketing Manager for the Company.

I did a scan and identified three possibilities. Then I interviewed them and sent up two candidates to the company as my final choices – with Choice 1 and Choice 2. A fortnight later the Chairman told me that he had selected Choice 2. I asked him why – and assumed it was the slightly lower emoluments that he was asking for, as compared to Choice 1. When I asked the Chairman he was delightfully vague! Imagine my amazement, when I heard through the Company grapevine that the Company had an astrologer on its rolls – and all appointments had to be approved by the astrologer. The birth date of Choice 2 was in sync with the company numbers and his appointment would be auspicious for the company.

Choice 1 was therefore not appointed to the assignment. And he never knew why!

Chapter 7

Filling in the Application Blank
It's the First Round

"It is best to do things systematically since we are only human and disorder is our worst enemy"

Most organised companies have a printed form, which they send to a candidate who has a chance of being called for an interview. It is called an Application Blank.

Generally, if you have received a printed form after you have sent your biodata, you can safely assume that you have cleared the 'preliminary round' and now, at least, you are being considered for an interview.

The printed form helps the company to have all the information they require in a certain sequence. This also makes comparison of candidates easier, especially if the analysis is computerised.

Most printed forms will specify that the form be filled in your own handwriting. If your writing is not very good, then it is safe to write in capital letters, with good black ink and no smudging. If handwriting is not specified, then the details may be typed.

Normally, a photograph has to be attached. Submit a reasonably good photograph of yourself. A print on mat paper, rather than glossy, is preferable.

You will also be asked to mention two references. These should be reasonably well-placed people, respected in society and who know

A complicated task – filling in the printed form

you fairly well. Your direct superiors in earlier assignments, who know you personally and professionally – will be ideal referees. You should ask them in advance if you can use their names as references, and confide to them what you intend to do, i.e. where you intend to apply and for what job. Courtesy requires that you keep your referees informed either by telephone or a short note, whether you have been successful in your application. It will then also be pleasant and easy for you to ask them to be referees again.

And a word of caution: Don't leave any blanks in the form in an attempt to withhold information. This never works.

Additional information is always welcome. If you want to elaborate, you can always attach an additional sheet to give further details on the brief remarks you may have included in the body of the form.

It is generally prudent to do a rough draft of all the details required in the form. Then keep it aside for a day. Re-look at it to see whether any answers can be improved. Re-check all dates, with certificates, to see if they are accurate. Only then, go ahead with filling the form. Make a photocopy of the form and keep it so you can refresh your memory about all the details given just before the interview.

Application Blank form attached

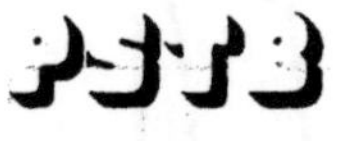

Personnel Selection and Training Bureau

APPLICATION FORM

205, Eric House, 16th Road, Bombay-400 071. India
Phone : 551 8027
Cable : MASCONS

Important : Please return form, along with a photo copy

FILE REF. No.

POSITION APPLIED FOR

TO BE COMPLETED IN INK BY APPLICANT IN OWN HANDWRITING

ATTACH PHOTOGRAPH

1. NAME IN FULL — BLOCK LETTERS (Underline Surname)
2. ADDRESS : LOCAL — Phone :
   PERMANENT — Phone :
3. BORN — Where — Date :
4. DOMICILE — Name State where you normally reside — Nationality
5. FAMILY — Are you Married — Number of Children and their Dates of Birth
   Father's Name/Husband's Name — Occupation (Present or Past)
   Father's Address/Husband's Address
6. LANGUAGES — Languages you speak Fluently
   Languages you Read
   Languages you Write — Your Mother Tongue
7. EDUCATIONAL QUALIFICATION

Exam or Degree	School, College University	Class & % Obtained	Year of Passing	Principal Subjects taken

8. SPECIAL ASSIGNMENTS — Mention here Details of Thesis Project Work, Special Assignments done
   Any Prizes, Awards won
9. SHORT COURSES IF ANY

Name of Institution	Period		Details
	From	To	

11. DETAILS OF EXPERIENCE : (Start with **PRESENT APPOINTMENT** and work backwards)

Name of Employer, brief Address and Nature of Business :	Date From-To	Each Designation held, the Period and description of major responsibilities (add. additional sheet if necessary)	EMOLUMENTS at start/while leaving gross p. a.

Present (p. m.) Emolument Details	Basic	DA.	HRA	Medical	Conveyance	Bonus	LTA	PPF	Gratuity	Pension	Others (Please specify)

12. PRESENT EMPLOYMENT

Name & Address of Employer :	Number of Employees : Annual Turnover :
Designation on joining :	At present :

Outline in detail your job responsibilities and product/divisions handled (Wherever applicable) (Please add additional sheet, if necessary) :

Through an Organisational chart, show whom you report to and who all report to you :

Give any information which would show why you are most suited for the assignment :

13. PROFESSIONAL MEMBERSHIPS	
14. HOBBIES & EXTRA CURRI CULAR ACTI-VITIES :	
15. HEALTH	State any serious illness you have had :
	Power of optical glasses
16. REFERENCES	Give Name, Address of two Referees (These persons must be resident in India. holders of responsible positions, and not related to you.)
17. PREFERENCES	What type of work do you prefer?
	Are you prepared to work any where in India?
18. SALARY	What total emoluments do you expect?
19. JOINING DATE	If appointed, when can you join?
	I hereby declare that the entries in this form are true to the best of my knowledge and belief. Date : Signature of applicant________________
NOTES OF INTERVIEWER :	Intelligence : Knowledge : Analytical Ability : Communication : Ability : Personality : Experience :

Chapter 8

Called for an Interview – You've Won the Second Round!

"The world stands aside for the person who knows where he or she is going"

If you receive a call to attend an interview, you have won the second round. It means that your initial application was well received and now the printed form has made you eligible for a personal meeting with the company's executives.

You've won the second round!

The printed form inspection is the screening process of the company. It tells them who they do not want because the applicant does not meet the basic specifications.

With the interviewing process, they will begin the selection process – deciding which of the candidates they do want.

It is like heats and finals in sports. You may not make it in the final selection but at least you have a fighting chance!

When you receive the interview call, you are expected to telephone the company or reply in writing, to confirm that you will attend the interview on the date and at the time specified. If you do not do this, then they may not expect you. This is something, which can cause unnecessary problems and misunderstanding.

Chapter 9

Mentally Preparing For the Interview

"The toughest thing about success is that you get to keep on being a success"

There is no need to get flustered when you get a call for a job interview. However, if it is your first or perhaps your second job interview, it may be a natural reaction to miss a heartbeat. Nevertheless, you can train yourself to look forward to a job interview with a mental attitude of pleasant anticipation rather than fear.

You can mentally train yourself to be sufficiently casual about the outcome of the interview so that you do not suffer from fear psychosis. A little nervousness is a good thing. It will make you taut, attentive and wanting to do your best, like in public speaking or stage action. Even very accomplished public speakers like Winston Churchill always experienced certain nervousness and a flutter in the stomach before they addressed a gathering. But too much of it can show in the blanching of the face, a trembling of the fingers, coldness of the hands, perhaps a stammer in speech and the mind going blank. All this can ruin the interview.

On the other hand some people are too casual. They will telephone and ask for a change in date and/or time because they have to play a football game or attend a music lesson class. Candidates who already have a job will telephone and ask if the interview can be held on a Saturday or Sunday because that is their weekly holiday. They assume that prospective employers have to keep open shop on their own holidays for the convenience of interviewees. This is something that will definitely go against candidates in an evaluation of their sense of purpose, seriousness about the assignment and, in general, about the total attitude.

A little nervousness is a good thing but too much of it can ruin the interview

It is not easy to strike a balance. Given a desire to learn and improve and a measure of self-discipline, you can train yourself to acquire the right mental balance. It is a balance between being over casual on the one hand and over-confident on the other. It is an attitude of being mildly nervous mixed with a pleasant anticipation where you would be disappointed (but not despondent) with an unfavourable outcome.

Whatever the kind of interview you will be attending, you are going to be asked certain questions. To be better prepared for the interview it would be a help to list out, some of the possible questions that you will be asked. The secret is to use empathy.– to put yourself in the interviewer's place and look from his perspective.

1. Think of the job you are applying for.
2. If you were interviewing someone for this position, what would you look for in the ideal candidate, and what questions would you ask?

3. How would the qualities essential for this job match your own SWOT analysis?
4. What do you need to ask yourself?
5. What do you need to ask the interviewer to know if the job is right for you?
6. How can you show that you are ideal for the job?

A Real Situation

I had sent an Interview Call letter to Fernandes, for the position of Group Product Manager, giving a notice of 15 days. He phoned me, just two days before the due date. 'Mr Vieira' he said 'you had asked me to see you on Tuesday, 20 June, at 11.30 a.m. Since I have some work at Navi Mumbai on Friday and will be passing your office on the way, could you please reschedule the interview for 9.00 a.m. on Friday so that I can then proceed for my business appointment?'

Our office only opens at 9.30 a.m. I was leaving on tour on Thursday. Fernandes just assumed that everyone will reschedule for his convenience. Naturally, Fernandes never made it!

Chapter 10

Physically Preparing For the Interview

"At an interview you have to present yourself formally and professionally. Remember looks may be deceptive but appearances count"

It is necessary to pay some attention to the physical aspects of preparing for an interview. You need not appear in your Sunday best but you should certainly be well groomed and dressed appropriately for the occasion. If you adopt the attitude of 'I don't care' and 'It does not matter these days' or 'I'm not a stuffed shirt', you will lose out on a very silly count.

Hair should be trimmed and neatly combed. Not everyone can carry off a Beatles look with aplomb! Depending on the job level, a shirt, tie and suit, or shirt, tie and jacket, or blouse and skirt, or suit is the norm. The blouse or shirt should be clean and well pressed, the collar and cuffs not frayed. Again, the trouser or skirt should be neat and well pressed – not too tight, not with flapping bottoms, and certainly no jeans, irrespective of the cost and the reputation of the hip-label. Make sure that there are no missing buttons, half opened zips or unsightly oil stains on clothes.

In general, interviewers like to see a person dressed fashionably but with a quiet moderation. There should be a certain neatness of person with fingernails and moustache (if any) properly trimmed. Shoes should be well shined and reasonably quiet, with neither the squeak of leather nor the stiletto jabs of high heels, even though the latter (with finely pointed toes) may be the current height of fashion.

And of course be aware of bad breath and body odour. This can be very offensive and can easily be corrected by brushing your teeth or

Prepare physically for the interview. Dress and behave appropriately. An 'I don't care' attitude won't get you anywhere

gargling with a mouthwash. Body odour can be overcome with the use of deodorants, especially under the armpits.

It is often true that when you are successful or somewhere in the higher rungs of the commercial hierarchy, you can take liberties with the way you dress and groom, and people will still listen to you and want to be with you. But at the entry point of a career, any major variations from the norm are looked upon with some incredulity.

Interviews have a strange laxative effect on some people. So go to the toilet before you leave for the interview. Sometimes, in spite of this precaution, you may still need to 'visit again' just before the interview.

Never have any alcoholic drink or smoke before an interview. Interviewers have sensitive nostrils, and they will detect the faintest tinge of gin, or beer, or nicotine on your breath. They don't take to this very kindly and you will be out on just the first impressions. Nor is it acceptable to be chewing gum during the interview however 'in' it may be in other company.

Then there is the question of assembling your papers.

1. A cut-out of the job advertisement,
2. A copy of your application,
3. A photocopy of the filled-in printed form,
4. The Interview Call letter,
5. Copies of certificates (degree certificates; leaving certificates from previous employers) and proof of other achievements. Company newsletters, sales bulletins, etc.

These should be placed in sequence in a neat folder.

Always carry a pen. Make sure it does not leak. Carry a good pen though it need not be and should not be a Parker gold. This will perhaps look ostentatious, and make a negative impact.

Chapter 11

New Methodologies in Screening
Telephone or Video Screening

"These days, you have to run fast, just to keep abreast."

Whether you are appearing for the first screening interview, in person or on the telephone, you will want to:

- create a positive impression from the start
- be mentally and physically prepared
- get to know the organisation
- anticipate questions and prepare the answers
- feel confident and composed.

With advances in technology, letters of application and the accompanying CVs are accepted online. You need to sell yourself in no more than two pages.

Now many companies screen their long list of applicants by using a telephone interview. The purpose of the conversation is to create a realistic short list for the next stage. Only a small number of candidates make it from this to the next stage.

Often a screening interview will be unannounced. The interviewer will ask you whether it is convenient to talk. It is a good idea to say No – and that you will call back. This will give you time to think of what to say, how to say it and create emphasis on points that you want the interviewer to remember. Generally a telephone interview will last 15-20 minutes. Be clear about whom you are speaking to and don't jump to conclusions.

On the telephone you can make an impact only with your voice. The interviewer cannot see you. Therefore, the great need for mastery over the six dimensions of paralinguistics – volume and tone, pitch and quality, speed and emphasis. There are two things you should always remember – be relaxed and smile. The smile gets transmitted over the telephone. Make your story interesting – and relate what you are saying to the role.

Some organisations are now using video conferencing for this screening. This makes it even more real than teleconferencing. You should not get put off by the technology. It is good to arrive early and become familiar with the surroundings and feel comfortable in facing a computer screen.

The general guidelines will always remain the same – stay calm; listen to the question; speak clearly and steadily; tell the truth; avoid talking too much; make it relevant.

A Real Situation

A senior manager screening for a key post in her division, rang an applicant to discuss some aspects of his CV. When he answered, he assumed he was speaking to the manager's secretary – and he was sharp and abrupt. When he realised that he was talking to his potential boss his tone and manner changed. But it was too late.

Naturally, he never made it to the next stage of the selection process.

Chapter 12

Setting Out for the Event

"A vision is where you are going; a plan is how to get there."

If the interview is in a different town, then try to arrive a day or half a day earlier and get to know the geography of the place, the bus routes and the location of the office.

Find out in advance how to get to the interview venue. It won't do to get lost

Even if the interview is in the same town where you live, it is prudent to go on a check visit to the interview venue some time in advance. You will then be familiar with the place and know how to get there. Perhaps you can even go right up to the reception room.

Confidence comes from knowledge. Therefore knowledge of the time it takes, the route, the location, even the face of the receptionist will give you a certain confidence, which will show through at the interview itself.

On the day of the interview, start out well on time. Leave sufficient time for contingencies – breakdown of the taxi, missing two buses, missing the connecting subway train. Arrive at the venue at least half an hour before the appointed time. Carry a book or magazine to read while you wait. If it is raining or likely to rain, it is a good precaution to be armed with an umbrella or raincoat so that you are not caught out in a heavy shower and then arrive for the interview late and dripping wet.

A Real Situation

Prepared for contingencies

Shyam had started out from Andheri, for an interview 20 miles away from the commercial district of South Mumbai. He was looking for a position as Advertising Manager in a large conglomerate.

He had allotted 2 hours for the journey. It seemed ample. He would get off the train at Marine Lines station in South Mumbai and go to 'Maker House', 2nd floor. When he actually got there, he could not find Calypso Ltd. Fortunately he had the Interview Call letter. And then he knew! The office was at Maker Chambers III at Nariman Point; three miles away! He rushed out and could not find a cab for 20 minutes. Then he got one and landed at the Calypso office five minutes after the appointed time.

Shyam went through the interview. It seemed to go reasonably well. But he never got the job. He always wondered whether it was the 'five minutes late' that changed his destiny!

Chapter 13

Lull Before The Storm

"Daring ideas are like chessmen moving forward, they may be beaten, but they may start a winning game."

Arriving a good half hour before the interview time gives you time to collect your thoughts and relax. You can give your name to the receptionist first, and await your turn at the reception area. Reading a book may help to take your thoughts away from the immediate encounter and hence help you to be calm and unfluttered.

If many candidates have been called and the disposal is quick, you can take a chance and try to meet one or two candidates who have finished and are on their way out, beyond the reception area, to find out about the interview environment, the kind of person the interviewer is, and the kind of questions being asked. This will help you to be better prepared for the encounter with immediate, relevant, and other people's hands-on experience.

And finally, when your name is called, take your folder and walk unhurriedly to the interviewer's room; knock before entering, remembering to shut the door behind you (unless it has an automatic door closing attachment) and walk towards the interviewer's table. You should not sit until invited to and then only in the seat, which has been indicated.

The greeting should be pleasant, but not too loud or bright: a warm 'Good-morning Mrs X' or 'Good afternoon, Mr Y. My name is so-and so' is sufficient. You should not offer to shake hands unless the interviewer offers his or her hand first. Keep your folder on your lap, not on the

It's important to remember your manners at an interview. For instance, entering the room without knocking could mean a bad start

interviewer's table or the other chair. A posture of respectful attention is most preferred – neither servile nor cocky; the head slightly forward in an attitude of attentiveness.

All this may seem unimportant to you but many interviewers will tell you that candidates who might have been otherwise suitable had lost out on the job opportunity because they had:

- entered the room without knocking
- insisted on pumping the hands of all five members of the panel without their invitation to do so
- entered the room with a cigarette between the lips (unforgivable)
- taken a seat without being invited to do so
- placed their folder or briefcase squarely on the table
- sat slouching in the chair, or crossed their legs in a manner which gave the impression that *they* were the interviewers
- asked for permission to smoke (which is reluctantly given) when no one else in the room was smoking or worse, when the table had on it a 'Thank you for not smoking' sign

- played with the pen, pencils or other items on the interviewer's table, perhaps unconsciously out of nervousness, but inexcusable nevertheless.

It is important to always remember that the interviewer is interested in you. After all, it is in his interest to get the right person. He is neither for you nor against you. It is therefore up to you to make sure that you do two things to maintain that interest:

- you should know how to differentiate yourself from all the competition.
  - by knowing more about the company/or the industry
  - by displaying more enthusiasm for the assignment
  - by throwing a few ideas of what could be done for further improvement (however, do not try to be too smart and cocky).
- you should know how to position yourself
  - as the closest fit between the job requirements and the talents/experience you have to offer.

❀❀

Chapter 14

The different kinds of Interviewers

*"The reasonable man adapts himself to the world;
the unreasonable one persists in trying
to adapt the world to himself. Therefore,
all progress depends on the unreasonable man."*

If you have managed to get some background on the interviewer from the other candidates well before the interview, this will help you to know what to expect.

If you have not been so lucky, then you have to be prepared to expect anything. As a preparation for this, you will have to study the different types of interviewers.

To begin with there are two basic types of interviewers

- the Inexperienced and
- the Experienced.

Inexperienced interviewers will start hesitantly as they are unprepared. They do not have a list of questions on which they will focus and they will interrupt frequently. They do not take notes and often ask misleading questions. Some may not talk at all while others talk too much. They will keep taking telephone calls during the interview, which disturbs the whole flow of the dialogue. They do not concentrate on what you say and do not know how to close the interview.

Inexperienced interviewers will have to be guided by the candidates – who have the responsibility to ensure that all the assets relevant to the job are brought out even though the interviewer may not have probed and given the opportunity to highlight these.

Please do not expect the interviewers, especially the inexperienced ones, to be totally in charge. This will force you to partly take charge of the interview and you will feel empowered.

Experienced interviewers start on a pleasant note and make the candidate feel at home. They have a list of questions to ask; they probe gently and ask open-ended and relevant questions. They listen attentively and are in control of the interview. They have instructed their secretaries not to put any telephone calls through. They take notes of relevant information and close on a pleasant and positive note.

Interviewers can also be classified under the following types:

The Egoists

They are so full of themselves and their own achievements that they spend most of the interview telling you how important they are and how they became so successful. They want to find out how much *you don't know* rather than how much you know. Because they are so over-confident and so 'cocky' they are generally unprepared. They need some fine tuned ego massage.

The egoist interviewer won't give you much of a chance to say anything at the interview

The Autocrats

They want you to be amply aware of who they are and of the immense power that they wield. They call the shots and others have to fall into place. They are generally well prepared. You should answer only what is asked. There is no need to greatly elaborate.

A Real Situation: Interviewing is an Art

It was my first interview for a job. I arrived at Glaxo, at Worli, Mumbai at 2.50 p.m. for the interview fixed at 3 p.m. I was on time – on a July day of torrential rains and flooded roads. I was ushered in to see Mr Ian Mckinnon, Purchase Director of Glaxo. My raincoat was dripping. My shoes were wet and I was clammy all over.

Mckinnon was at the door to receive me. Although, I was appearing for an interview for the position of Management Trainee and he was a Director on the Board, he took my coat and hung it up. He offered me a seat and reduced the air-conditioning. He asked for my preference – tea or coffee; then waited till his secretary served us both with steaming hot cups of tea.

Very tentatively he began a casual conversation – but I knew he was following a plan. "You don't mind if I take a few notes?" he asked. And I said 'No, I don't mind'. The conversation went into details of my college days and seemingly wandered into a discussion of Indian dance forms and temple architectural styles in the North and South of India. We talked about books and drama, and likes and dislikes. He told me briefly about his family and asked about mine. I had not realised it was 5.45 in the evening when we came to a close. It was not as if he hastily brought the interview to a conclusion. He closed it smoothly and saw me off at the door. Forty years later, I still remember Ian Mckinnon and my first interview, with nostalgia. It has never happened again, in the same way, with the same elan and style!

The Democrats

They like to have nice casual conversations. They will speak and also allow you to speak. They ask open-ended questions and they are intent listeners. They want to hear other opinions and are open to other, perhaps conflicting views, that are not their own. They generally end up making friends with many of the interviewers. They are always well prepared.

You should not be taken in by the courtesy and convert the interview, into a social chat. Don't lose sight of the fact that you are at a formal interview for a job in the organisation!

The Laissez-faires

They are the ones who do not know how to begin. The interview will begin virtually like an accident start. There is no plan, list of questions or note taking. The interview meanders along like a river without a firm riverbed. These interviewers are pleasant, friendly and warm, but it may still not end up as a good interview because they are unprepared and generally lose the direction of the interview.

You need to take partial charge of the interview right from the beginning; and guide it along the lines you want to.

The Whiz Kids

They are experienced and well prepared, perhaps too well prepared. They know a lot and want you to know that they know a lot. They will deluge you with questions and will laugh gleefully when you don't know some of the answers. They establish their superiority, not in the same manner as the egoist or the autocrat but in a kind of indirect cerebral way.

You need to stroke their egos, without yourself appearing to be a fool. This is a delicate balance to work out.

The first Impressionists

They make up their mind immediately. They are experts on the human personality. They can size up a person in one glance; study the character by the shape of the eyebrows, fingers, and jaw. They can assess people by the way they dress, the kind of pen they carry or the way they talk. And irrespective of the questions asked and answers given, they have made up their minds. They "know" people – or think they do.

You need to make a good first impression. Your grooming, attire and deportment will count here in greater measure. Once again, a little stroking of the ego will go a long way!

An aside

The former salesman was appearing for an interview to join the army. The Sergeant asked him "What were you doing earlier, Brown?" I was a salesman. "Good. You will get plenty of orders here!"

Chapter 15

How many Interviewers will you face?

"The journey to excellence is a journey; not a destination"

Many interviews on a one-to-one basis are conducted by only one person. For the interviewer, such one-to-one meetings are the easiest to organise and for the interviewee, they are the easiest to face. The plus point of such interviews is that they give the interviewer the advantage of talking to the candidate in a direct manner with eye-to-eye contact.

Imagining that your interviewers are dressed in nothing but their underwear may be one way to help you overcome your nervousness

At some interviews there may be two people – one from the Department concerned and the other from the Personnel Department (perhaps a psychologist).

It is necessary to identify them and get to know their names. You can then connect the person to his or her role in the interview. It is necessary to face both of them. Include both within your eye span, although you should maintain direct eye contact with the person asking the questions at any particular time.

There could also be a panel interview where three to six people constitute a panel. They may all represent different disciplines in a company. You have to deal with them in the same way as you would in the case of two members.

A Real Situation: Changes in Strategy

Dan was Director, Finance and Personnel of the Copco Company. I was therefore surprised when Singh told me that he had been interviewed twice by the CEO, Nolan, and should be getting his appointment letter early next month for the position of Personnel Manager.

'But did you not meet Dan at all?' I asked him. 'Was Dan not on the interviewing panel?' He should have been, since the position of Personnel Manager reports the Director, Personnel.

I was sharing my surprise with Ken, the Production Director. With greater experience in the ways of the world, Ken was able to see through. He said 'Walter, when Singh joins he will report directly to Nolan and not to Dan. The interview is an indicator of the shape of things to come.'

Ken was right. When Singh joined, there was a circular signed by Nolan the CEO, that the Finance and Personnel functions will now be separated and made independent. Singh will be in independent charge of the Personnel function and will report directly to the CEO!

The important thing is not to get flustered in facing so many people. Just keep your cool and imagine they are all one person.

Also, if two or three ask questions in quick succession, don't try to answer them all at once. Deal with one interviewer at a time, beginning with the first person who asked.

If you do get nervous when facing a group of people at a panel interview, it is recommended that you follow the technique used by 'prisoners of war' during World War II. They looked at their interrogators and imagined they were in their underwear or worse, completely nude. This made their tormentors look ridiculous and it gave them confidence to face them squarely. Sometimes it gave them so much confidence that they laughed and their interrogators certainly did not find that funny. But the interviewee's objective was achieved!

Chapter 16

Are Interviews a Sure Way for Best Selection?

"It is important to do the right things than to do things right"

For interviewees, it is important to go well prepared and give your best. If you have done this and find that you have still not been selected, remember that interviews are certainly not a guarantee of best selection.

Many surveys have been done in the past to check whether two different interviewers with similar qualifications, background and experience would select candidates in the same ranking. They don't. One sales manager ranked a candidate twenty-fifth while the other one ranked the same candidate first. Both asked similar questions but formed different impressions. Their perceptions were so different as to have a gap from 1 to 25.

Therefore, for those interviewing, interviews give a guideline and a direction in taking a decision on the suitability of a candidate. But this must be used together with intuition and experience; and most important, with references from reliable and relevant referees.

A Real Situation: The First Impressionists

'Did you see the shape of his fingers?' the CEO, Raj, asked me. I said I had not. 'They are club shaped and short. Not a good sign. Such people are ruthless.'

Raj had made up his mind in the first three minutes. Nothing that Sam said during the interview made any difference. Sam did have a lot to say. He had a record of success. But it did not matter. Sam was not selected. Raj insisted that he should not be and this was based on the shape of his fingers!

Chapter 17

A Question of Time

"It is terrible to speak well and be wrong"

The greatest constraint in an interview is time. If a large number of interviews are to be conducted, then the pressure becomes even greater. Therefore, both the interviewer and the candidate, have a responsibility to utilise the limited time to maximum advantage.

Many interviewers make the mistake of not knowing what they are looking for. They are confused and this is reflected in their questions and in the final selection. The whole interviewing exercise becomes an exercise in futility.

The first thing interviewers need to do is to write a job description (what is the candidate expected to do?). From the job description, interviewers can derive a job specification (what is the candidate expected to know in order to do this job?). From the job specification, a brief 'Person Profile' can then be derived which will be used in the advertisement. This brief but specific profile will be a great help in attracting the type of people that the interviewers are looking for. Clarity about the Person Profile will thus help reduce the time taken for the interview.

Candidates will have to help save time by matching themselves against the Person Profile, as given in the advertisement, and sending an appropriate application.

Later, they will complete the application blank (sent to them by the company) in all respects and clarify any seeming ambiguities in the form itself (e.g. why there was a break of two years during the graduation studies).

An ill-prepared interviewer may talk endlessly about himself rather than getting the candidates to talk about themselves

The application blank should be filled clearly and neatly with those aspects of academic qualifications and work experience (relevant to the job applied for) highlighted. Candidates should first make a draft of the answers they will give in the application blank and fill it only after they are sure of all the facts - dates, grades, etc. They should also keep a photocopy of the application blank so that before the interview (if they are called) they can recheck all the facts given earlier.

The corporation should also play its part in saving time and ensure that the interview is conducted by the appropriate person. Ideally it should be the person to whom the candidate will report. In addition, each candidate may be interviewed at the same time or separately by someone in Personnel, who will look at the 'personnel aspects' of the candidate. If the job is senior enough, some more interviewers (perhaps the Directors) will also want to interview each candidate. If the whole schedule is worked out clearly in detail, and well in advance, it can help considerably to reduce wastage of time.

There will be very little time wasted if the interview is a properly planned one. The interviewer will try to find out how much you know rather than how much you don't know. Interviewers who have thought out in advance, about how the interview is to be conducted will ask questions designed to make candidates talk in some detail about themselves. They will rarely ask questions that can only elicit 'Yes' or 'No' answers. Such close-ended questions will rarely allow interviewers to get to know how a candidate thinks, or if he thinks at all! Questions inviting one-word answers can also lead to long silences during the interview, which are bound to discomfort candidates and make them more tense and uncommunicative.

There can be group interviews in some cases where a group of applicants are put together and given a subject for discussion in a limited time period. They are observed by the interviewer who does not interject but remains an observer. The strategy here is to ensure that you participate so that you make a valid contribution to the discussion, which will help to progress the discussion. Trying to dominate and wrestle the leadership, or keeping totally aloof from the goings-on, with a disdainful half smile playing on your lips, are both to be avoided.

Chapter 18

The First Impression : The First Stage

"Match your image of yourself to how others see you. Keep in touch with their reality."

There is an old saying in the 'Art of Selling' that the attention-getting stage is the most important stage of a selling interview because:

- what you say in the first few minutes decides the customer's attitude towards you and
- the customer gives you more concentration in the first few minutes than at any other time during the interview.

The way you speak will have a lot to do with the first impression you make on others

Therefore the first impression is important. As mentioned earlier, care has to be given to good grooming and neatness. The battle is half won with a good start. At this stage, the state of health of the interviewee will not be dwelt upon. But it is a plus factor when you appear healthy, and the interviewer can judge and gauge this by the way you walk, your posture, the paleness or rosiness of your face, the way you talk and the way you sit or slouch! Of course, at a later stage, the successful candidate will be sent for a medical check-up.

A Real Situation: Appearances Matter

I was interviewing candidates, with the Managing Director of a large German transnational. The position advertised was Vice President – Finance. We had finished three interviews and we were waiting for the fourth and last candidate to enter the Board Room. Based on the Application Blank, he seemed to be the best candidate.

Mehta entered and he was waved into a seat. The interview began. It was after ten minutes of smooth sailing, that Gunther noticed that Mehta had a very large thumbnail. It looked grotesque. We were both too polite to ask him why he had allowed that nail to grow. But he was outstanding in his work record. I phoned Mehta the next day at his residence and told him that a 'nail' stood in the way of his getting the assignment'. He agreed to cut if off. The problem was solved. The Company got the right person. Mehta got the right job.

The clarity, tone and strength with which you speak will also determine the impression you make on the interviewer.

Do a quick check on yourself:

- Do you speak so softly that interviewers cannot hear you or have to strain to hear? They may ask you to repeat a few times - but after that, will either give up or cease to care.
- Do you mumble or speak too fast?
- Do you vary your tone to make 'hearing' pleasant?

In some jobs, like those of salesmen, receptionists and telephone operators, speech can be a critical factor in the interview process. For others like accountants or planning assistants, it may not be as important.

But since verbal communication is necessary in every field, while dealing with customers, employees and colleagues, it is wise to devote time and effort towards improving your skills in this area. ■

Chapter 19

After the First Impression : The Second Stage

"It's only the people with push that have pull!"

If appearance, health and speech are acceptable, then the interviewer proceeds to the other aspects like education, intelligence, experiences and progress.

Education

This would have been stated clearly in the application blank itself - the degrees acquired, in what subjects; the grades obtained; special merit prizes won; extra courses done.

However, in the interview, the interviewer will try to find out the scope of the curriculum and the comprehension and recall of at least some of the basics of the subjects covered.

If the job requires more technical or specialised skills, then the questioning on the subject will be deeper and much more exhaustive, and will be conducted by a technically competent interviewer.

Intelligence

The assessment of your intelligence is normally based on the replies you give to various questions on topics which may be as varied as local politics to environment planning.

However, in some situations an IQ test may be conducted for the candidates. IQ tests should not create panic in the candidates. They should be conducted only by trained psychologists. It should also be remembered that IQ tests are only indicators and not a final ranking scale.

Some companies have trained psychologists to conduct psychological tests like:

Sentence Completion Test

A sentence is left incomplete and you are asked to complete it.

Ink Blot Test

In this test, one is asked to interpret various blots of ink.

Picture Story Test

A story is required to be written by the candidate based on a picture shown.

Progress

Most interviewers want to see what progress the candidate has made in his working career. Has he moved from a salesman of one company to being a salesman of a smaller company - or of an equivalent company? Has he moved up the ladder, not necessarily by promotion but at least by increased job content, or bigger clients handled?

Progress in previous work experiences is something interviewers like to see in the CV

Some candidates seem to either regress or remain stagnant over a long period of time and they have no explanation for it. They fail to meet this criterion for progress.

Experience

The interviewer will try to find out the length and breadth of your experience – what you have learnt from the jobs you have done. It can be the same experience repeated every year for ten years, or it can be a wide range of experiences over ten years. Interviewers would prefer the latter because it is not just experiences in selling but selling of different kinds of products, to different kinds of customers, in different geographical areas, which constitutes a broad spectrum of useful experience.

Of course, if you have just come out of college and have had no previous work experience, then this part of the interview becomes superfluous. If you have done part time work in college, or taken holiday assignments, this will add to your experience portfolio.

A Real Situation: Right Experience Counts

Randhir had applied for the position of sales representative with a large consumer durables company.

Atul, the sales manager, asked Randhir whether he had sold anything at all during his years at college. He was surprised with what Randhir told him. When he was in high school, Randhir had been breeding gold-fish for tanks and selling these to his class mates. During one summer holiday, he sold melamine tableware, house to house. During another holiday, he did promotion for a brand of water purifiers at petrol stations. During another holiday, he was a market research investigator for a brand of industrial lubricants.

Atul was impressed. Randhir had a wider range of experience than some of the others who had been in the full time work force for three years. Randhir was selected for the assignment.

Chapter 20

The Third Stage : Attitude, Integrity, Perseverance and Motivation

"To listen closely and reply well is the highest perfection we are able to attain in the art of conversation"

This is the most difficult stage of the interview because all the four facets cannot be easily isolated, or quantified. That is why multiple interviews help because then the interviewer has enough time to get to understand the person better.

Attitude

This can only be assessed by indirect questioning. Any direct questions will only bring out the obvious answers. Psychological tests will also give an indicator to bear out or refute the interviewer's impressions.

How do candidates talk about work, the hours of work, the family, the kind of work they did in their earlier companies or about their earlier bosses?

If they speak badly about all of them or some of them, it will reflect on their inability to get on with colleagues or their basically hostile attitude. If they speak ill of their past employer, (even if it is true) they are the kind of people who will also talk unkindly about you when they have left your employment.

Integrity

This can also be assessed only by indirect questioning. Candidates cannot be asked whether they are honest. They will say they are, and they may not be. Why did they take five years to do a four-year degree course? Why did they get such low grades? Why did they leave their last job without another job in hand? Why did they record such low sales in their earlier job? Ask such questions.

Answers to all these will give a clue to their integrity. The first clue, of course, is when they fill in the entire application blank, answering every question no matter how unfavourable the answer may be to the candidate.

Multiple interviews give the interviewer an opportunity to ask the same questions, again and again, to find out if there is consistency in the answers given.

Perseverance

Do candidates have the ability to stay on in spite of difficulties? What do their academic records show? What does work experience show? Is a candidate only looking for the highest salary for the lowest effort? Does a candidate want to be a contributor or just a passenger?

Interviewers also try to look for integrity, motivation and perseverance in candidates. They want someone who will work hard in return for what the company gives

Motivation

What turns a candidate on? Is it only financial motivation or does non-financial motivation matter? Are they doing some evening courses, correspondence courses or self-study courses to improve themselves professionally? Do they have the drive to want to get somewhere? How is their leisure time spent? What kind of friends do they have? Are they self-motivated or do they need someone else to constantly motivate or goad them on?

Integrity

'What are your hobbies?' I asked Karl. It was towards the end of a very satisfactory interview. Karl seemed to have all the qualifications and experience for the job we had advertised for. He was pleasant and conducted himself well. I just wanted to get a feel of his life outside work.

And I was surprised at the strangeness of the answer. "I collect hotel knives and forks," he said. It is an old hobby. "I pick up a knife and fork from every hotel I stay in, in India or abroad. I have a very large collection, it is all neatly marked and identified."

This was done without the hotel's permission. Karl did not pay for the cutlery he was taking. In fact, he was a petty thief!

That did it! Karl was not selected. There was a large question mark in the box for Integrity!

Contacts do not always help

Kris was one of the candidates who had applied for the position of Sales Promotion Manager. His father was a well known physician and a friend of my father. Two days before the interview Kris' father phoned my dad to say that his son had applied for this position and he was being interviewed by me. Could my father please ask me to do whatever I can to get Kris into this job?

On the appointed day, Kris walked into my room when he was called. He was dressed in casuals, as if going on a picnic. He wore sports shoes without socks. 'Hi, Walter' was his greeting. He took a seat without being asked to. Kris leaned back and lighted a cigarette. 'So what is this job all about, Walter?' he asked.

All through the interview his attitude was condescending. It looked as if he did us a favour by coming for the interview. It will be a bigger favour, if he accepts the appointment. I went through the interview as best as I could. The 'cockiness' was giving me high blood pressure. I brought the interview to a fast, unhurried end. Kris was not selected!

An example of Perseverance

Vasant was being interviewed for the position of Administration Manager. He seemed to meet all the requirements very well. As usual, I was moving towards the end of the interview with my standard questions of 'Tell me Vasant, what are your hobbies?'

And Vasant leaned forward to tell me 'Mr Vieira, I really had very little time for hobbies these last twelve years. I used to play hockey and football when I was in school. But I went to morning college and worked during the day, during the 8 years when I did M. Com and Law. After that for 4 years, I got permission from the CEO to stay back every day till 7 p.m. at the office, to go through all the correspondence in the Central master file, so that I could know what's going on in every department of the organisation. I also lived at Borivli since I could not afford a spacious house closer to downtown. It would be 10 p.m. by the time I got home. There was just enough time to rest and start again in the morning! But the 4 years of Master File education was worth it. It taught me more than any college curriculum could have taught me. I felt the pulse of the organisation."

We selected Vasant. Here was a man of grit and determination. An example in perseverance! Years later I met him again. He was Chief Executive of a medium sized multinational. He had made it all the way to the top!

Job Satisfaction is a big Motivating Factor

John was an engineer from IIT, Mumbai and did an MBA from IIM, Bangalore. This was a good background and he was immediately picked out on campus recruitment for a Big 6 consulting company in Mumbai. It was a good assignment, which involved assessments of executive remuneration and work in this area for corporate clients.

After just 18 months, John quit to join a Software Company in Bangalore at 60% of the emoluments he got from his earlier company. What made John do this? He wanted challenge; a lack of routine; new problems to solve everyday; the informality and autonomy of a 'go-go' successful Software company with amorphous hierarchies and matrix teams constantly forming and re-forming based on needs. He did not mind the lower income. He wanted much more than income. He wanted job satisfaction through an obvious personal contribution. This is what motivated John. ■

Chapter 21

Dealing with different styles of Interviewing

"The better you think you are doing, the greater should be your cause for concern."

It requires a lot of disciplining and study to come through successfully at interviews of different kinds.

If the interviewer is an *egoist* who keeps talking about himself, you will have to humour him, and perhaps flatter him. It is easy to identify the egoist by the number of times he uses the 'I'. 'I have been so busy' he will tell you. 'Every problem in this Company seems to land on my desk'!

A good way to go along with the egoist is:

"Tell me, Sir, how did you go up so high at such a young age?"

'Indeed Sir – there does not seem any part of the country where you have not worked.'

At the same time you must make sure that the interviewer gets to know something about you. You must emphasise the qualifications and experience, which are relevant to the job. Before the close of the interview, make sure that you summarise the important points again so that the interviewer will remember you and all your strong points.

Never contradict an egoist and don't argue. Perhaps you can disagree pleasantly if the topic is important enough and overlook it if it is not important. But don't cross swords.

If the interviewer is an *autocrat*, you will identify him immediately by his tone, his posture and the rough and brusque language he uses. You should then be adequately submissive, without being servile. Your manners must be totally above board. Don't venture into asking for permission to smoke and don't smoke, even if permission is given to you.

Interviewers will sometimes be difficult and demanding just to see how you will react. Don't lose your cool

Correct sitting posture is even more important in this situation. Give answers to the point, without being too brief or terse, and yet without expanding on them. If you feel expansion is necessary, then always ask, "May I elaborate on that further?" or "If you permit me to talk on that part further…?" Give interviewers the commanding position – but don't be too servile as they will be critical of you if you seem like a person who can be kicked around. So somehow, you will have to strike a balance between being submissive and assertive.

If you meet a *democrat* you will identify him by his controlled and pleasant manner. It is easy to distinguish a person who respects another human being as a person; rather than as a title. If you meet a democrat, you are lucky, as you will be made to feel at home and relaxed. Perhaps your interviewer will start with casual conversation and a little humour.

You can certainly be free and frank, perhaps even contradict pleasantly and expand on any point. You need not be overly particular about your sitting posture, but at the same time make sure that you do not take liberties and appear cocky.

If the interviewer is a *Laissez-Faire* you could be in trouble. His air of carelessness can make you too comfortable. It can be a pleasant meeting, which gets you nowhere – a kind of dating with no marriage in mind. You will therefore have to help in conducting a good interview. Your interviewer will not know how to start because he has no plan. You will have to take the initiative and give information in a systematic, organised way, perhaps give your interviewer a summary sheet of why you are best qualified for the job. You may even have to help to bring the interview to a smooth and positive close.

If the interviewer is a first impressionist this is a great challenge. It is not easy to identify first impressionists. They will go through the whole interview process for perhaps one hour, but they would have made up their minds in the first few minutes and you do not know it. It is better to get some information about first impressionists in advance. It is necessary to study their facial expressions and their eyes. It is necessary to be careful right from the time you open the door. However, beyond that there is little that you can do except to tailor your presentation to the requirements.

The panel of interviewers could be composed of all the five types of people and you have to be truly adept at handling all of them at the same time. It is important to include the whole panel within your eye span all the time. You may focus on the person who asked the question (at a time) but the eye span must include all of them in the conversation. Any member who secretly (and perhaps unjustifiably) feels that he or she has been ignored will cast a 'No' vote against you, later, and this can be easily avoided by taking early precautions.

❁❁

Chapter 22

What are the tough questions at Interviews?

"If you can keep your head when all about are losing theirs...."

Rudyard Kipling

Do you have some skeletons in the cupboard? Don't worry. We all do. Interviewers will generally try to trip candidates on these difficult questions – sometimes in a planned manner; sometimes unknowingly. It is always a good idea to list out these tough questions and also work out the answers you will give.

Some of these uncomfortable questions will be on

- gaps in the sequence during education
- gaps in employment
- knowledge of the technology or the industry
- any health problems
- reason for many changes in employment
- relationship with past superior and colleagues
- reason for change now.

You need to master the skill of checking with the interviewer that you have understood what has been asked – like "Let me understand. You are asking me..." or "you want to know how I would..." or "You feel that I have made too many changes, as one too many...let me explain." Such rephrasing gives you time to think and to respond. You need to be cool and confident and reply positively. The Interviewer also wants to see how you react to pressure.

They say some of the toughest questions are those that give you enormous scope like:

- Tell me about your career to date.
- What are the highlights of your career?
- What are the goals you have set for yourself?
- What have been the three major achievements in the last three years?
- What have been your major failures and what have you learnt from them?
- What changes in the environment (in the last 5 years) have affected you and how?
- How much do you think you are worth?
- If you did get this job, how long will you stay?

In answering these questions, you need to project the strong points of your personality and your strengths – and in that process, show that you are well matched to the organisation and the job. It should seem to them that you are the ideal candidate to be recruited.

Always make sure that you connect what you have done in the past; to what you can do in the future. And thus contribute to the prospect company. Depending on the context, you may refer to –

- improvements made; turnover and/or profits increased; people managed; projects completed; savings made; budgets managed; problems overcome.

Also remember that you will be asked how you spend your leisure. You must have a good answer in response to an enquiry about hobbies. This gives the interviewer an overview of a balanced personality. But if you are one of those who has no hobbies at all – do not bluff. You will be caught out.

A Real Situation

The late Prakash Tandon, first Indian Chairman of Levers, India, told me that he was once interviewing a candidate who seemed very well qualified – a tripos from Cambridge – but yet seemed superficial. So he asked him what his hobbies were – and this 23 year old said golf and reading.

Tandon then asked him what books he had read in the last three months. He could not name one. They he asked him what did he read at all – and he replied that he read the Illustrated Weekly and the Readers Digest!!

He was caught out. Naturally, he was not hired!

Chapter 23

Making the Interviewer want to Buy

"A good salesman is not just a glib talker. He tries to meet the genuine needs/wants of the customer"

You as an Interviewee have to be careful of how you project yourself. Hard sell seldom succeeds at interviews. Interviewers get suspicious of candidates who seem too eager to join and who do not show a certain reserve. Such candidates convey the message that they do not have any other alternatives except getting the job perhaps because they are jobless at the moment.

Unless you have just finished college, and are therefore free, you should not offer to join immediately. If you are working somewhere else, you should state your notice period and the time you will need to tie up loose ends, after which you will be free to join the new company.

If there are some aspects on which you are not clear – the level of entry into the company; the exact designation; to whom you will report; whether any career path exists; the details of the company's incentive scheme – make a request for another meeting. Take your time and be clear about what you want to do and what is expected of you.

Some candidates tell lies, in an attempt to sell themselves. Instead of saying that they have not passed their exam, they state that they have passed and then cannot produce the certificate.

They may also say that they have a driving license (when they don't); that they have achieved a certain sale in the territory (five times more than what was actually achieved); that they know well the two referees, who are very eminent people, (when they know them only very slightly), or that they are earning a certain salary (which is a highly inflated figure).

Exaggeration and hard sell seldom succeed at interviews. Don't force yourself on the interviewers, try a more reserved approach

This bluffing cannot take you very far. At some time, you will be asked to produce the certificates, prove sales figures, or reference is made to the referees.

Some candidates exaggerate in an attempt to impress. They may talk about how they played in the senior team in college (which might have been exactly twice in a year) or took part in various public speaking contests which they won (perhaps once). Some exaggeration is permissible and can pass unchecked but the experienced interviewer can easily distinguish the possible and the probable.

A certain reserve combined with enthusiasm and genuine interest in investigating the suitability of the assignment, without any over eagerness projected through, is in order. 'When will you take a decision?' 'Do you want me to contact you again sometime?'

A Real Situation

The Managing Director of a pharmaceutical company was interviewing Gopal for the position of Marketing Manager. Sometime through the interview, when all the preliminaries were over, and the in-depth interview had begun, the Managing Director asked him what the sales were of a recently introduced product and the promotion budget. Gopal excused himself. He said he knew the figures, but could not disclose them. It was 'in company' information. The Managing Director asked him what plans the company had for new introductions in the next few years, considering the difficult economic climate. Again, Gopal said he could not answer him. The Managing Director seemed visibly upset over such a "non disclosure attitude." The interview ended on a pleasant note. But Gopal did not get the job. He had been discreet and it did not pay off.

On the other hand, Sam in a similar situation at an interview, did tell the interviewer a good deal about his Company's plans and recent achievements. All he needed was a little encouragement and he came out with all he knew. Sam did not get the job either. This Managing Director felt that Sam would be as forthcoming with company secrets after he joined the organisation as he is with the secrets of his present company.

Chapter 24

Controlling the Pace

"A moderate and steady pace, gives the best car mileage"

To a large extent, the interviewee can control the pace of the interview. It does not matter whether the interviewer is an egoist, autocrat, democrat, laissez-faire or first impressionist. It does not matter if questions are asked in quick succession by different members of the

With proper handling, you, the interviewee, can control the pace of the interview

panel even though you might not have begun answering the first question asked. It does not matter if multiple questions are asked, where two or three questions are hidden in a single one.

It is for you to

- remain cool and not lose your balance
- repeat a question so that it is clear to you
- rephrase a question aloud, to arrive at the correct meaning
- speak softly and clearly after some thought, irrespective of the speed with which questions are asked
- maintain your composure even if there is a period of silence either because you have yet to begin speaking, or the interviewer is thinking through the next question.

Undoubtedly, all this comes with practice, but it helps if you are conscious of it right from the start. With the unprepared, untrained interviewer, it becomes more necessary for the interviewee to control the pace, if the interview is not to flounder, by being too rapid, or by having long silences during which time both interviewer and interviewee are just looking at each other.

By controlling the pace and sometimes slackening it, you must take care not to lose the interviewer's attention and your control over the interview. The secret again, is in maintaining pleasant eye contact even through the uncomfortable silences.

Chapter 25

Close the Interview on a Positive Note

*"Talking and eloquence are not the same:
to speak and to speak well are two things.
A fool may talk, but a wise man speaks."*

If you have controlled the pace of the interview, you can play a major role in bringing the interview to a close. Of course, a close which is entirely dictated by the candidate would seem presumptuous: 'If there is nothing else you would like to ask, may I say good-bye?'

An ideal close is where both interviewer and interviewee cooperate and jointly come to a finale:

- 'Are there any other questions you would like to ask?'
- 'No, I think I have asked all I wanted to know.'
- 'After listening to you, I feel even more interested in this assignment than I did earlier and would be happy to accept it, if you find my profile matches your requirements.'
- 'No, I have got all the clarifications and it certainly does make me feel very interested.'
- 'Thank you Mr Roy, for your time. I hope we will meet again.'

Something like this sets the mood for the closing and also conditions the interviewer's attitude just before he or she fills the evaluation form after the departure of the candidate.

Don't appear too eager at the end of the interview. Leave with a pleasant smile on your face. Interviewers will prefer such candidates

Again, don't be too eager. Don't ask whether you will receive a reply within 15 days; or whether you should phone up after a week or a fortnight. Leave in a pleasant unhurried manner, with a smile on your face, the same way you came in.

And don't forget to close the door behind you!

Chapter 26

How Candidates Pay Heavily for Poor Manners

"Good manners is only showing consideration for others"

In early 2000, there was an interesting article in Marketing News of USA, which gave a listing of all the complaints that employers had about interviewees. It was a time before 9/11; and a time when employment in the USA was at a 30 year high. It was a world of stock options and salary increases. Yet, one recruiter described this period as "when bad things happen in a good economy". Here is a list of comments made by employers, which will provide guidance to interviewees:

- Candidates can be cocky in this environment.
- Source of today's entry level employees who are GenXes, looking for their first jobs, take too much for granted, displaying an arrogance that often costs them a job offer.
- This is not the case with senior level employees because these people are more realistic. They were there to see and experience Black Monday when GenXes were still in high school.
- It's the stupid stuff that really irks interviewers. There are applicants who don't check the spelling of the human resource contact's name, don't proof read cover letters, fail to write thank you notes and even forget to get directions to the interview site.
- People say 'I forgot a copy of my resume' or they say they will call on such and such date and 95% of them do not call when they say they will.
- And technology hasn't helped either. Candidates still don't use the spell check programme on their e-mails, they rely so heavily on

the automatic tool that they don't notice when the programme substitutes one word for another.

- I place a lot of openings on Master.com and other sites. I can't tell you how often I get responses from people with email addresses that are out of date and they haven't put in any other way in which we can get in touch. I think you should put all your contact information in your email.
- They send me attachments, such as resume or work sample, in a format that I can't open.
- They don't do their homework on the company to which they have applied. Thanks to the INTERNET, most companies have a site. It is silly not to check that.
- Write follow up notes, even if you think it didn't go off well. You have a chance to make a lasting impression with a follow up note. Even if you don't want the job, you don't know where the interviewer will end up next.
- There are increasing numbers of candidates starting a job search, not because they are unhappy with their present position, but just to see if the salaries and perks they hear about at the gym really exist.
- A lot of people just come looking so they can get a counter offer. Sometimes they even go so far as to accept a job, only to renege on their commitment. This kind of being untruthful is really inconsiderate of a lot of peoples' time.
- Everyone now have multiple offers, so you get candidates who are wishy-washy on what it would take to get them to take the job. I get them to specify the salary, allowances, vacations and the start date. But then, when I present that offer, it's not a done deal. They want $ 50,000 until they hear someone else got $75,000. Some candidates are not holding up their part of the bargain.
- Almost every hiring manager has been burned by a candidate, who accepted an offer, only to turn down the position days before his start date.
- There have been candidates who, a week before they were scheduled to begin their new job, sent an email to say they 'found another opportunity'. An email! They don't even take the time to make a phone call. They don't realise that one day 'this is going to come back and bite me.'

- Entry level applicants have inflated self worth. I run an internet company and I get all these resumes that under 'skills' people put – knowledge of Netscape and Internet Explorer, Windows and email. That's good. Do they know how to use the phone, too?
- A lot of young people are not looking to work that hard. One young man when told that the work day at the new firm started at 8 a.m., said he did not want to come in until 8.30 a.m. He said 'Eight o'clock is not conducive to my lifestyle.'
- The most common complaint among hiring managers is inflated salary requests. We recently had an applicant with just six months work experience asking for a salary of $ 70,000 and a new laptop. Young people are making demands that more seasoned people are making.

A Real Situation

I was one of a panel of three. We had just finished a three hour interview with Roy. It was hard work for us and for him. This was the last of three interviews for the position of Country Manager for a large UK based corporation which was a leader in its field. The vacancy had arisen, because the present CM was being promoted as Regional Director in Singapore. Being a very young company, there was no one completely suitable, available to be promoted.

We were all relieved to have found a suitable candidate at last. Roy seemed to fit the job description as if tailored for the role. We thought we should celebrate. The Chairman who was visiting brought out a bottle of rare whisky and offered us a drink.

This was very welcome. The conversation became social and engaging – the atmosphere was friendly. Roy finished his drink very fast, while we were still less than half way through. The Chairman noticed this and requested him to help himself. Roy poured himself an extra large and rejoined the conversation. By the time we finished our first drink, Roy was half way through his third. He left after a fourth drink – mumbling his goodbyes to each of us.

The tide had turned. All of us looked at each other. Each knew what was in the other's mind. It was a unanimous decision earlier that Roy should be appointed. Now it was unanimous that he should not be!

Chapter 27

Emotional Quotient Becoming A Critical Parameter

"There is more to life than the IQ factor"

It is true that there is no scientific formula that guarantees a successful hire. But a structured approach and clear knowledge of your requirements can help you avoid pitfalls in the hiring process.

As we go along, there is increasing opinion that we need to look at emotional competencies more seriously when making critical selection decisions. Too many companies select executive talent on the evidence of attributes that can be learnt over a period of time – like technical skills. They tend to look at factors like education, IQ, and track record but fail to probe the elements of emotional intelligence: willingness to learn, ability to work in a team and cultural fit.

The performance of a multinational had slipped and its systems needed to be re-evaluated. The Company required a country manager with an excellent technical orientation in order to put the company back on track.

The company evaluated several candidates and zeroed in on an individual with very little experience in a multinational environment, reasonable academic pedigree, considerable technical expertise and heavy 'star' tag.

The new manager began well. However, within a few months he showed signs of slowing down. His approach didn't work too well with domestic and international colleagues. Slowly the incumbent became isolated and he resigned within a year – some even speculated that he was asked to go.

By disregarding emotional intelligence in the hiring process and ignoring the aspect of organisational fit of the candidate, the company overlooked a critical success factor. This incident substantiates the result of a study conducted with 500 managers across three continents that unsuccessful managers failed largely due to their low levels of emotional intelligence.

Chapter 28

And perhaps now, a Psychometric Test?

"There is a never ending search for exploring new horizons"

A news report recently warned: "If it's IT you're looking at, you'd better be a team player; if it's BPO, ensure you're stress hardy. Companies no longer hire just about anybody and everybody, nor are ability and knowledge the key determining factors."

The right people with the right attitude – that, increasingly, is the focus at IT and BPO (business process outsourcing) companies. And organisations are ensuring it stays like that by engaging a new breed of selectors – psychologists – for effective selection of employees.

Psychometric of behavioural assessment is taking centre stage in the new age selection process. Software giant Microsoft is giving a lot of weightage to behavioural attributes for selection of the initial batch of professionals for its upcoming BPO centres in Bangalore.

Texas Instruments, Dell, GE, AOL and Siemens are all porting psychometric tools into their personnel selection process in India. Psychometric testing has been used by defence establishments worldwide since World War II, and is now finding favour among corporates.

It is said that "Psychometric assessment completes the selection process along with ability and skills/knowledge tests. This is the current buzz in the BPO industry, where the call agent has to demonstrate a great deal of patience and empathy while handling a customer call."

Many organisations have painfully discovered that traditional ways of selecting candidates for new-age job roles involving high stress and high risk can lead to problematic post-hire outcomes.

An agent in a call centre should possess attributes such as ability to handles stress, empathy for people and a high degree of tolerance. An IT professional typically requires to be a team player; open to learning, self-satisfaction and friendliness.

With the recent emphasis on 'emotional intelligence' as a prerequisite for successful job performance, many organisations are turning to procedures evaluating candidates for positions in terms of their personality characteristics, interpersonal style and job-specific aptitude in order to maximise job success.

Chapter 29

Reviewing Your Performance At The Interview

"A man who has committed a mistake and does not correct it is committing another mistake"

It is always a good idea to review your performance after every interview:

- What were the questions that were asked?
- How were they phrased?
- What were the answers given?
- What was the reaction to the answers?
- Could you have said anything else?
- Did you come off too strong or too weak?
- Was there a problem of communication? Language?
- Could your tone have been improved at different stages?

Make notes of your observations. Think about them and practise to improve your weak points. Use these notes in future interviews so that your performance improves constantly.

This does not mean that you should be a professional interviewee constantly looking for jobs and attending interviews. But you will have many opportunities to attend interviews, perhaps for promotion within the company or perhaps you may get to a stage where you will need to be an interviewer yourself. Then these observations will be helpful.

Chapter 30

The Interview As A Public Relations Exercise

"There is no such thing as an insignificant improvement"

Gone are the days when the interview was a kind of miniature Spanish Inquisition with the interviewer sitting on a pedestal in his hooded glory, looking down at all the common folk.

Both interviewee and interviewer can't afford to antagonise each other. This is a time to exercise all public relations skills

A Real Situation

It was one of my first job interviews, after I graduated in pharmaceutical technology and Mohinder S was the Production manager of TFC Pharma. He was a retired Army Brigadier who had taken a job in the civvy-street, but acted as if he was still in the Army.

Mohinder sat back in the Chair and grilled me on technical skills and on attitudes and general knowledge. Of course, he knew little of the technology – and this came through. He knew the theory of interviewing – but his attitude was of Officer and sepoy. It was something that I resented. He had asked me whether I smoked. Since I said yes, he asked me for the brand, which I told him.

Towards the end of the Interview, he made an offer with what I thought was a paltry sum even at that time in 1961. Since he had made a spontaneous offer, I also responded spontaneously and said "No – thank you. It will not fit my requirement."

It was then that he made a mistake. He did not follow the rule in Selling 'Never be insulted by a refusal" He felt insulted! So he responded with 'Perhaps you will have to smoke a cheaper brand of cigarettes Mr Vieira. Your ambitions are too high for an entry level job'

A few months later, I joined Glaxo (20 times larger than TFC) at that time) as the first Management Trainee in India. Six years later I was a Manager and Mohinder and I were representing our respective companies at association meetings. He knew, who I was, and I had not forgotten him. After one of these meetings I picked out my cigarette packet. I told him I continued to use the same brand. He said he was not surprised considering my rapid climb up the corporate ladder.

Mohinder could have acquired a friend at the interview who could have become a collaborative colleague at association meetings. But he did not use the Interview as an opportunity for a PR exercise!

In an age of fast and great change, all of us must recognise that many of those who were down, when we were up on our way up; are may be on their way up when we are on our way down!

Today, an interview is a public relations exercise where the interviewer and interviewee become acquainted and perhaps remain on nodding terms, irrespective of the outcome of the interview. Social and commercial mobility is so high today that the person you interview today may be interviewing you 15 years later, depending on where both of you have arrived on the Snakes and Ladders playing board of life.

That is why neither the interviewer nor the interviewee can afford to be offensive, impolite and inconsiderate. The candidate may not be given the job at the end, but if a patient and attentive hearing at the interview has been given and a courteous letter of regret sent after the decision has been made, the candidate will think well of the company and the interviewers.

It is possible that the candidate is or will become a customer of the company's products or services, or a shareholder. Either way, the candidate will be a happy person with pleasant memories of a brief encounter.

Chapter 31

Refinements in Interviewing Techniques

Many companies now use an Intelligence Test at the entry point in the organisation. They may also use various psychological tests as mentioned earlier, like a Sentence Completion Test, an Ink Blot Test or Building a Story (based on a picture shown) Test. Trained psychologists conduct these tests and therefore, it is only the larger corporations, which will use such test methods.

If the candidate 'feels' right to the interviewer, then the job is most likely to be in the bag

A Real Situation : Folly of Making Individual Judgement

The CEO – Nik was dynamic, young, result-oriented and successful who reached the top of the executive pyramid by the age of 40. But he was also an astute politician – unfortunately in a negative sense.

Nik decided to bring in an outsider to head as Director, the marketing function. The company had two marketing managers – handling each of the two divisions and any of them could have been promoted. But Nik wanted to be "clever".

He advertised under a box number and got the kind of response box numbers will always attract for a senior position (poor!). He screened the best from the mediocre. Also he began the selection process with interviewing. Arun was finally selected. He had impressed Nik that he was the Consumer Product King of India. After all, had he not established Everest snow cream and many other products?

It was after just three months of Arun joining that his real worth was evident. It was nowhere near what he was paid. There was an overall lowering of morale in the marketing department. The two Marketing Managers left in disgust. The Product Managers and Sales Managers left soon after. Nik faced Gomorrah – a barren city destroyed by fire and God's wrath.

Nik had made a fatal error. He had tried to use an individual judgement. He should have had a panel; multiple interviews and watertight references. He got too cocksure and the organisation paid a heavy price!

Some companies use group discussions as an important part of interviewing. However, group discussions can only be used in the case of junior level, or at best, middle level jobs. Senior personnel cannot be subjected to such group discussion interviews although there are some companies, which try to do this.

Finally, an interview remains an interview. All these psychological techniques are only supportive. They can provide pointers, but the final decision is always based on the 'feel' of the interviewer. This 'feel' can only be improved by developing greater objectivity - finding out what the candidate knows which is relevant to the job; having multiple interviews and opinions of more than one interviewer; making notes for future reference; and making checks with the referees.

Chapter 32

New Ways Interviewers are looking at Interviewees

The Verbal Interview

There was a time when hotel lobbies were overflowing with job aspirants, waiting their turn for an interview. This may soon become a thing of the past. Voice resumes, the latest technology that many companies will soon adopt – will cut the cost of hiring and do away with logistical hassles for corporates.

Business communications solutions provider – Avaya Global-connect has developed a solution aimed primarily at companies in the IT/ITES sector and in banking-financial services. All of these do large scale hiring. The new solution will reduce costs, increase the quality of hiring and reduce physical travel.

Avaya developed this program because they found that most candidates did not measure up in communication skills. So what was the solution developed? When candidates apply to a company a mail is sent asking them to call up a certain number. Then, with the help of an interactive voice response platform, the candidate is asked questions. The interview is concluded after asking the candidate to read a passage provided. The results are immediately forwarded to the HR team for assessment.

This new procedure developed by Avaya, enables companies to significantly speed up hiring – and check on the candidates' communication abilities without asking them to travel all the way to a particular city for the interview. It saves huge costs for all the candidates and the company.

This new system is a boon, especially to the IT, ITES, Insurance; Pharma, FMCG companies who recruit in large numbers across a broad geographical spectrum.

Pre-Employment Networking Site

www.bravenewtalent.com is the world's first pre-employment networking site. It is a new way of connecting talent with potential employees. This platform enables students and other young job seekers to take control of their careers by creating professional profile and connecting with their desired employers. Social networks are used to connect with friends. Talent networks are used to connect with prospective employers. Employers thus see well in advance, those wanting to work for them, thereby allowing them to develop their talent Radar and reach potential employees at a much earlier stage.

In years gone by, companies used to observe the trainees they got on summer vacations from technical schools or B schools. Having worked for two holiday sessions, corporates would then decide whether they would want the candidate on a full time basis or not. Brave New Talent has made this process faster and more compressed. Signs of changing times – faster, better, cheaper!

Extensive Background Checks

The most important virtues employers should look for in any candidate are honesty and integrity. These are inherent traits. All other traits can be acquired. Pre employment screening is one way of getting close to understanding the person's profile on such accounts.

With a few major scandals in the BPO industry recently, companies would rather delay a recruitment rather than skip over the process of reference checks. Pre employment screening services is a boon to IT/ITES/Insurance/Financial Services companies, which are recruiting people every day and perhaps, every hour. Thus the 'Background Check Procedure' has become a very critical part of the recruitment procedure. In fact, in many companies, every necessary check is done, before calling the candidate for an interview.

Pre employment screening was traditionally done by the police – but is now most often purchased as a service from small private businesses that specifically render such services. Information usually includes past employment records, credit worthiness and criminal history. When a corporate out sources this service, they often have a clear SLA – Service Level Agreement defined. The check includes background checks; employment verification documents; reference checks; character and personal reference checks. Some companies also ask the Agency for checks on performance on the job, ability to work with teams, integrity, leadership quality, ability to take tough decisions, commitment and areas of development, which may be a deterrent to a prospective employee's performance.

Interviewers and their organisations can benefit greatly from such an employee screening program – decreased turnover, reduced expenses and elimination of risks of theft and fraud are just some of the advantages. Even for employees it creates a safe and secure environment. It makes it so much easier to practise integrity as a value in all their actions.

Listening to the Voice of the Interviewee

This is now the latest. Organisations everywhere know the importance of brand ambassadors. No matter how much money they spend on brand initiatives, they know that it is the employees who can really take the organisation forward in terms of branding.

However, existing employees are not the only ones who can act as brand ambassadors. These can also include prospective employees who come for interviews or tests in the organisation. The impression they have of the organisation is powerful because these candidates go out and share their experience with people outside and this can be many, many people.

The President of one company says: 'We want to make sure that the whole interview process is a good experience for the candidate. Even if the person does not get an offer from the company, he must leave with a good impression of the organisation. It is a long term relationship with the candidate!'

And for this to happen, everyone from the receptionist to the HR Manager has to be trained to make the candidate feel comfortable within the office premises.

Many companies now have feedback forms. Some even have one-to-one discussions. The feedback from the candidates is carefully assessed by an internal team of the company and if there are any valuable suggestions that could improve the recruitment process, it is implemented promptly in the system.

Such feedback has helped companies to change the timings for interviews to make them more convenient to candidates; to provide maps to easily get to their offices; to give feedback to the interviewee, on why he was not selected. Thus an Interviewee's feedback to the Interviewer, about the recruitment process itself can be a win-win for both. ■

Chapter 33

Little Things which Make a Big Difference at Interviews

*"The only boundaries we have are in form.
There are no obstacles in thought."*

There are many small things, which are generally overlooked, but these make a big difference at interviews.

These things are not difficult to master, as can be seen from the following:

Chewing gum and smoking may annoy or appall your interviewers, and it may cost you that job

Smile: Most candidates forget that entering a room with a smile, is more important than entering with a suit on.

Good manners: This can be seen in little things like closing the door behind you; pulling a chair out without making much noise; taking a seat only after being invited; exhibiting and maintaining an attentive posture; not smoking or chewing gum.

Quiet Confidence: This can be revealed in the gait, the posture, the holding of the head, the way you use your hands, what you keep doing or not doing with your hands.

Chapter 34

Interview Preparation and Checklist

Here are some of the questions an interviewer might ask and which you should have the answers to:

Family Background

1. What does your father do for a living?
2. Does your mother have a job as well? Where?
3. How many brothers and sisters do you have? What do they do?
4. In what towns have you stayed? Which towns did you like? Which did you not like? Why?
5. What was life like at home?
6. Are you planning to move out of home?
7. Are you planning to move out of town?
8. Are you planning to get married? When?

Education

1. How did you like school? Why did you change schools?
2. Did you like the school? Why?
3. Why did you go to 'X' College?
4. Why did you choose these subjects?
5. Do you think that your grades reflect your correct ability?
6. What games did you play? How proficiently?
7. What extra curricular activities did you participate in at college?
8. How will your qualifications help in the job you are applying for?
9. If you were to live again, would you go through the same educational process?

10. Which subjects did you like most? And least?
11. Did you do any courses outside regular hours?
12. Did you pursue studies while you worked?

Work Experience

1. Why did you take up this kind of job?
2. Why did you join and leave these companies?
3. What do you like most and least about your job?
4. What was your major contribution to your company? Was there anything significant that you did?
5. How many people reported to you? Who did you report to?
6. How did you get on with your staff and colleagues?
7. What are the problems you face in your industry or company?
8. Why are you looking for a job change?
9. What kind of contribution do you think you can make?
10. Why do you think you are suitable for this position?

A Real Situation

Romy had spent twenty-four years in the engineering industry. He was at the Vice President level. But he was now keen on changing the industry focus. He wanted to get into the automobile industry, which he felt was a 'sunrise' industry.

Romy spent four months reading all he could about automobiles - the market in Europe, India and US; the market shares; the strengths and weaknesses of each brand; the problems of infrastructure, et al. Then he applied to the two new automobile entrants into India.

Romy was surprised; he was called for an interview by both companies. He came through with flying colours. It seemed he knew more about the automobile industry than some of those on the panel.

He was offered a good assignment - and he accepted the offer. Good preparation had led to a predictable result!

Aspirations/Attitudes/Opinions

1. How do you judge the progress you have made so far?
2. Has it been an increasing learning process? In what way?
3. What are your aspirations?

4. Where do you expect to go in the next five years?
5. What growth opportunities do you anticipate in your present organisation? Why?
6. What growth opportunities do you expect here? Why?

Before you go for the interview, prepare yourself for all the questions you may be asked. That way, you'll always be forthcoming with information

7. What do you know about this organisation – its management, style, products, and policies?
8. What circumstances have gone against you in the past?
9. Have you been under much stress? How have you handled it?
10. How did you get on with your boss?
11. Why have you not named him as your referee?
12. What is your connection with the referees named?
13. May we refer to them next week?
14. Do you feel comfortable working with figures and with computers?
15. Are you an outdoor person or an office person?
16. Do you prefer a staff function (more mental-planning) or a line function (more active-outdoor)?
17. Do you consider yourself a good communicator? Why?
18. Would you be better at verbal or written communication?
19. List one failure in your job. How did it help you? ■

Chapter 35

If You Get The Job

If you get the job you had applied for, and are happy to accept, write promptly accepting the offer, confirming the date when you will start work (see sample letter below). If you do not acknowledge the offer, it would seem you are uninterested and the offer could be made to someone else!

Before you start your new job, make a list of things you need to know about the job. Then, after joining, get yourself fully involved in doing 'a great job,' and thus, justify your selection.

SAMPLE OF A JOB ACCEPTANCE LETTER

16th January 2008

Dear Mr ________/Mrs

Thank you for your job offer dated __________, which I am happy to accept.

I confirm I will start work on 9th February 2008 at 9.30 a.m.

Looking forward to joining your Organisation.

Yours sincerely

Jennifer Lee

A Real Situation

This has never happened to me before and I hope will never happen again.

I had been responsible for the final selection of a Personnel Manager for a large multinational pharmaceutical company. We went through the whole process and finally selected the Deputy Personnel Manager of a large consumer product company. He seemed to meet all the criteria. He agreed to the salary terms and the date of joining.

I was surprised that he did not report for work on the appointed day. I thought it very strange. That evening I phoned his residence – and did that very reluctantly. It was on the odd hope that the candidate had perhaps met with an accident or something tragic had happened to keep him from meeting his commitment.

Imagine my shock when he answered the phone and told me in a very cavalier fashion "Oh, I'm sorry Mr Vieira. Didn't you get my message left on your recorder five days ago? I had already informed you I will not join you. You see, my company has offered me a posting in Hong Kong for three years. They did not want me to leave them. They have also given me a substantial increase which matches your offer. I therefore decided I will stay here, since I have been in the company for five years."

There was no apology – no remorse. It was so casual. I felt shattered that a Senior Manager could have such a sense of values – or lack of it. On reflection later, I was glad he did not join our company. We could do without such amoral individuals in our team. It was however a great inconvenience. We had lost six months – three months in the selection process and the three months notice period that he had to give his company and which he had asked for!

Chapter 36

If you Get the Job...but

It is likely that you may encounter some problems after being selected for a job.

Problem A

You had earlier attended an interview where you were told a decision would be taken at the end of two weeks. Later, at another interview, you

You've got the job but you want to have your cake and eat it too. What do you do?

are offered the job on the spot but you prefer the first job. What do you do?

- Accept the second, and forget about the first?
- Turn down the second offer, in the hope of getting the first?
- Explain the situation to the first company and ask if they could give you their decision sooner?
- Request the second company to give you a few days for your decision?

Problem B

You had applied for two jobs and were selected for the first job, which you joined a month ago. The second company finally makes a decision and offers you a better deal - a higher designation and more money. What do you do?

- Resign, since you have not yet been confirmed?
- Explain your predicament to your present employer and inform him or her that you are changing for a much better offer?
- Turn down the new job, as it is unfair to leave the present assignment, so soon and so abruptly?
- Use the opportunity to improve your situation in the present company by showing them you are worth more than they are paying, as the new offer indicates.

Problem C

You are currently an accountant with Company X, which is a small-sized company. You have recently been interviewed for the post of Accounts Manager with Company Y, a much larger organisation. When Company Y makes an offer, you find you are offered the lower designation of Asst. Accounts Manager, though the salary is 10% higher than what you are getting now. What will you do?

- Accept the offer on the grounds that the salary is higher?
- Politely decline the offer on principle, because the job applied for was "Accounts Mgr.?"
- Explain to Company Y that there could be an error as you were interviewed for a higher position?
- Don't reply to the offer in sheer annoyance?

Solutions To These Problems

These are dependent upon each individual, the circumstances and the moral values he or she holds. ■

Chapter 37

If You Don't Get The Job

If you don't get the job, then it is necessary to analyse why you failed. There is no need to feel despondent or heart broken, or lose confidence in your own self-worth. Only one candidate can be selected out of the many that have applied. There could have been someone just marginally 'ahead' of you. You may have been under-qualified or, as it sometimes happens, you may be too good for the job.

If you keep on failing at interviews, find out why. Is it because you're not suited to the types of job you apply for?

If you fail at perhaps three or four interviews, do some introspection to find out why you keep failing. Is it that you apply for jobs for which you do not have the qualifications and/or experience? Then, you are applying for the wrong jobs.

Doing the following exercise would be a help:

1. What post was the interview for?
2. (a) What were the good things that happened?
   (b) How did you feel?
3. (a) What were the things that went wrong?
   (b) How did you feel?
4. How could you have handled the interview differently?
5. What positive steps can you take to ensure success at future interviews?

A more detailed analysis would be:

- Was your initial preparation adequate?

It's not the end of everything if you don't get that job. Keep at it – at some point, you will succeed

- Does your initial approach put off the interviewer?
- Are your answers incomplete, unsatisfactory or unconvincing?
- Do you argue with the interviewer and differ in opinions in an unpleasant way?
- Do you get diverted so that you cannot highlight your strengths and perhaps, only your weaknesses come through?
- Do you speak too softly, so that much of what you have to say is not heard by the interviewer?
- Do you appear too keen to get the job?

If you do this kind of introspection after every interview regret letter; if you study all the hints that have been given in this book and use them in combination with your own wit, intelligence and tenacity - at one point, you will succeed – YOU MUST!

Anecdotes

By Mr A K Agarwala
President
Hindalco Industries Limited

In the process of recruitment of candidates, both at junior and senior levels, to a very large extent, organisations have to depend upon interviews. Different tools and techniques have been devised by organisations to make the process of recruitment somewhat more stable and credible. However, whatever the process, the interview is an essential part and perhaps, the concluding part in making appointments.

What does one look for in a candidate in interviews?

Depth and extent of his knowledge; his ability to apply his knowledge and expertise; his attitude; his ability to adjust to a new environment and the degree of flexibility and the capacity to carry people along with him. In addition, the style and values of the candidates also are crucial. Also the manner of their presentation.

Since the candidates tend to show their best face, it is necessary for the interviewers to look behind what the candidate appears to be or seems to say at the interview. Unmasking the candidate is very essential, otherwise the selection process may suffer from a halo effect.

After having seen many candidates both at junior and senior levels over a period of time, I am of the view that recruiting people particularly at senior levels amounts to investing in Hope and only the action performance of the candidate in work situations can show whether the selection was right.

In one case relating to strategic recruitment at a very senior level, the selection board was thoroughly impressed by the intellectual acumen of the candidate, his dynamism, his past record and his achievement motivation.

On his joining the organisation, however, the candidate almost immediately put away his mask and started behaving in a quixotic manner, finding fault with people and all the processes of management. He made it absolutely clear that the organisation must adjust to his whims and he would not show any adjustment at all. The team building process was thus completely disrupted. The result was that he could not make any significant contribution and he had to leave the organisation after a short time.

Another case which comes to my mind is where a very accomplished academician, a Professor in Management in a prestigious university abroad, was selected to join the Commercial Department of a growing organisation. He had contributed a lot of papers to various prestigious journals and his articles were full of erudition and complexity. However, he could not apply even a part of his theoretical knowledge to the actual activity in which he was employed. This is again because he was a poor team builder and perhaps had chosen to live in an imaginary world and had no intention to adapt himself to the framework of commercial reality.

Contrary to these examples where the candidates had done exceedingly well at the interview, another candidate came for interview for a junior position years ago. He seemed to be thoroughly dull and unsuitable for any managerial position. He was given a routine activity in which dealing with people and money was involved. Over a period of time he learned all the tools of his trade and constantly added various skills to enhance himself and add value to the Company. He has continued to handle this highly critical but low profile assignment with ease and proficiency.

All the cases referred to above point out only one thing, viz., that the interview is only a means to probe the personality of the candidate and find out how well he would be fit in the new organisation. At the most, the interview is therefore an exploration and one cannot be certain about the outcome.

Organisations have to learn to look into the details of the candidates critically and for that the interviewers should carefully prepare for this. For example, going through the bio data of a candidate requires a special skill, a lot of patience and deep insight. Similarly while talking to a candidate the interviewers have to be quick in catching the points of strengths and weaknesses. While competence is essential in a candidate, the interviewers must also look for a positive attitude. A candidate lacking a positive attitude does not deserve to be hired.

Similarly, the candidates in order to be successful at the interview must be good in their line of specialisation, should have adequate knowledge and should have almost an inexhaustible capacity for learning and application of their expertise. Also, they must have good communication skills and a positive attitude.

The process of interview I have observed is an odyssey both for the interviewers and the candidates-both must continue to remain on the path of learning and application.

By Mr Kalyan Banerjee
Ex Chairman
Exim Bank of India

Led Up The Garden Path

Romesh came to the interview for a General Manager's post with great hopes. He was apparently willing to do and say anything that would please the interviewers. However, he underestimated the interview technique of the Chairman of the interview panel who opened the proceedings. Consider the reactions of Romesh to the Chairman's questions.

Chairman: "Romesh, I do not agree with those who argue that inflation is bad for India. What do you think?"

Romesh: "I fully agree with you."

Chairman: "I think inflation is good for India, because prices tend to rise which increases producer profits which get distributed to workers and various economic constituents, leading to general prosperity. What do you think Romesh?"

Romesh: "I agree, Sir."

The interview developed in this vein and Romesh was led into a deep mire from which he could not retrieve himself when the other two interviewers contested the position, in support of inflation, that Romesh took. Romesh apparently took that position in his eagerness to get into the good books of the interview panel Chairman, not realising that he would have to defend his position with other contending panellists. The panel Chairman was clearly leading Romesh into a "trap" from where Romesh did not recover. Romesh not only lost his prospects for a General Manager's position but also looked like a dog's breakfast, at the end of the interview.

The moral is that an interview candidate must take a rational position and not a position only to please. A rational position may not always seemingly please but at least can be defended on rational grounds. Every employer looks for rational employees with strong analytical skills, at the minimum.

By Dr Ranjan Banerjee
Ex Vice Chairman, Hindustan Lever Ltd
Chairman, Lintas Limited
Director, Consindia Pvt Ltd

Interviewing – Some Cases

Dressing for the occasion

In Hindustan Lever the selection of candidates has always been taken very seriously. In the early years when Englishmen were heading all the top and senior level functions, even dress was considered to be of importance.

The occasion was one of the first interviews for the selection of full-fledged Technical Management trainees. I was a young junior level manager at our Calcutta factory, but perhaps because of my technical qualifications, it was felt that I should be invited to join the Selection Board mainly as an observer but also as a resource person if needed. The panel was headed by the Chairman, Mr Hoskyns Abrahall and included the Technical Director, Mr Steve Turner and the Chief Engineer, Mr Richard Brown.

As we entered Mr Abrahall's room – he noticed that Mr Turner was not wearing his jacket. He turned to him and said "Steve, it is customary on such occasions to wear a jacket" – to which Mr Turner retorted "And why not a top hat as well?" and sat down. The matter ended there and so did the wearing of jackets, I think.

The Reluctant Candidate

Ever since its inception, the Management Training Scheme of Hindustan Lever has attracted many promising candidates. Every year there would also be pressures from various sources including top levels in Government. On one occasion it was strongly recommended that we take a young man who was the relative of a VVIP. Since there were some protocol problems as well as our own desire to be scrupulously fair, it was decided that I should personally screen the young man.

At the appointed time the young man sat across me in H.L. house. I commenced the interview but I noticed after a while that he was extremely uneasy and stiff in his response; so I stopped and asked him if anything was wrong. "Yes," he said "May I first ask you Sir, as to why you are interviewing me at this preliminary stage when I am told that as Personnel Director you sit in only at the Final Board. Is it because I am the President's grandson?" I replied that that was so. "In which case" he said, "I do not wish to carry on. I do not want any favours." I then assured him that there need not be any worry on that count; I would be scrupulously fair and would not hesitate to tell him if he were unsuitable. He quickly relaxed and we had an interesting interview at the end of which I told him that I did not think management was up his street.

A broad and relieved smile spread across his face. He never wanted to be a manager; he wanted to be a physicist – but strong family pressures egged on by top officials had made him apply.

He left smiling, thanking me profusely and a few months later sent word that he was happily pursuing physics at a renowned American University.

The "Controlling" Candidate

A Unilever Senior HR Management Course was being held at Jakarta (Indonesia) covering all companies in the Asia Pacific Region. As a principal member of the faculty, I was particularly asked to handle the Recruitment & Selection sessions. In this, I had decided to include a period for role playing on interviewing skills.

I had asked the Indonesian Company to be ready with a real life candidate for a final interview by a panel of selectors from among the participants. The rest of the course members would watch the proceedings and after the event, there would be a critiquing session.

At the appointed time, I met the candidate in an anteroom for a briefing session. The person turned out to be a stunningly attractive lady, a divorcee in her early thirties with a dazzling presence. I told her that she should be entirely natural because this was in fact going to be her final interview. She was being seen for the post of the Head of the Market Research section, which had just been set up.

As she walked into the Selection room, there was a stunned silence. The Chairman of the Board, the Indonesian HRD Manager began the interview but within ten minutes or so the lady had sensed a weak spot in his armour and responded with a flattering remark about his deep insight into the subject and how thrilling it would be to work with such gifted compatriots. The tables had turned and she now took complete charge of the interview for the next half-hour or so. All the selectors were gleefully answering her questions and responding to her comments. They discovered nothing of her competence but she found out a lot about them.

After a brief discussion following the interview she was unanimously selected. You can imagine the critiques that followed and it would not surprise you either to know that she did not last long in the Company.

The 'Halo Effect' Manipulator

This was in recent times and I was interviewing a candidate in his late thirties for the post of a functional head in a medium sized company.

He was not faring as well as I thought he would from his biodata. When I came to his "other interests" at the end, I found he had written "Reading and Wildlife." Since "Wildlife" is one of my major fields of interests, I warmed up to him and asked him how this interest had been kindled and whether he had visited any sanctuaries. "Of course" he said with a grin "I have been to Ranthambhor twice but I could not see any lions at all." I told him that was not surprising because there were no lions at all in Ranthambhor. He turned to me this time with a sort of pitying style and said, "Sir, Ranthambor is famous through out the world for its lions."

Needless to say the interview ended there. The young man had obviously been told of my interest and decided to try and use what is called the "Halo effect."

By Dr Vinayshil Gautam
(Founder Director-IIM(K)
Dalmia Chair Professor of Management
IIT-Delhi

Top level selection

As I reflect back on my several years of sitting on selection committees, I do find it possible to distil some common features that lead to a positive evaluation of the candidate and to their selection. There are also certain traits, which if they appeared to be a part of the candidate's personality, led to disaster. I need to confess that in addition, there were experiences in selection which I did not understand then and do not understand still.

To get the full import of what I am saying, it needs to be communicated that in my reflections I cover a universe of organisations, which were commercial in character (worth at times several thousand crores of rupees) and their board level appointments, identification of vice chancellors, not to overlook the selection of executive directors of commercial banks. I choose not to cover my experience in interviewing for management trainees, MBA, students and PhD candidates. The segment I am talking of is the top level in any given sector.

A common trait which I found, which went well across the board, was the ability to be clear, precise, and adequately informed of the job the person wanted. Additionally a candidate's sound reality touch with his own competencies helped. To aspire for a leadership position, the ability to grasp what is being asked and to anticipate what it would lead to, is critical. I also noticed that the better read candidate performed superior to the candidate who fancied himself as an 'operations' man.

Obviously, there are nuggets of anecdotes which I recall. They have their instructive value.

For the several years for which I used to sit on the committee to identify Executive Directors of nationalised banks, one question which I had occasion to ask often was the question "How much time do you find to read?" In one case, the candidate replied, "I come to work at 8, leave office at 8, where is the time to read?" Another candidate replied, "I am an "operations" man. RBI keeps sending guidelines, we keep following them. Where is the need to read?" (This was some 10 years ago). I recall telling the concerned Deputy Governor with the Reserve Bank then, "I think some of our banks are heading for trouble." If he had any reactions to what I had to say, he did not show them. I am no astrologer, but my forecasts came true.

That apart, I need to state how in a strange way, I found interviewing for an organisation as an excellent process of organisational evaluation. One gets to see, as through nothing else, culture and the ethos of the organisation, through talking to its people in interviews. The interviewer, if he is duly oriented, knows exactly what to plough to get to more sustainable conclusions.

At the senior position, a truly successful interview is one at the end of which, both the interviewer and the candidate has a feeling of joy at a very invigorating conversation.

Of course, more than once in a while, one comes across a glib talker or a person given to posturing or worst of all, someone who believes he can talk through to cover some major failing he would rather not reveal. All along, I try to be scrupulously correct but to the person who believes he has got away with all because of his ability to talk, I have been even more polite than what would be common to a normal conversation!

At the end of the day, quality does show and no matter what the grapevine would have us believe, by and large the committees, on which I have sat on, have been fair. A little tilting this way or that has taken place only when other things between two candidates have been by and large equal. There have been cases where somebody failed to get in when there were elements in his candidature, which made it somewhat of an ambiguous case. But a clear case seldom suffered.

Even if it is so difficult to keep one's peace with candidates who give you the feeling that they know so much better than what is being asked and wonder to themselves why they have to face an interview at all! I did not understand this attitude when faced with it and I do not know how to make sense of it still.

By Mr R Y Gaitonde
Chairman
The Gaitonde Group

We were looking for someone to organise and set up manufacturing units for leather products. We had to set up the factories for manufacturing products in keeping with the Government's policy to support value added product industries. The man who was chosen for this purpose did a good job in setting up the factories. This was a success. He had the ability to get people to work towards deadlines. Having set up these factories this man was made the head to run them. This was a mistake because he did not have the ability to organise manufacturing. He had no idea of cash flows, inventory controls and cost controls, anything to do with manufacturing. The result, he almost failed these beautiful companies he set up as per the vision of the Chairman.

The other incident was, we were looking for two Accountants, one for operations and the other for internal audit. These were filled up. But there was yet another accountant who was interviewed, who besides having a good knowledge of accounting, had also worked overseas in Africa and the Gulf.

Although, he did not have hands on experience in running the factories, he could advise those, in-charge of operations where they were making losses and where they were making profits. Since we were looking for a manager for running the leather garments and the leather accessories factories we thought we could have an accountant to head these units. We were disappointed when this man was not able to handle people because of his overpowering egotism. But once he got the hang of running the factories he saw where things were going wrong.

With his accounting background he was able to locate areas where the business was losing. He had his eyes on profits and with this at the back of his mind his purchases became more cost effective. He simplified production through various processes to cut costs. He made use of the inventories that were not moving to make articles that could be sold for profit in the local markets. He located people who had dead stock on hand which he converted into products for export and in various ways that he adopted he turned the company around from a loss making one to a good profitable one.

By Jamshed J Irani
Managing Director
Tata Steel Ltd (TISCO)

"When I have interviewed persons I have always paid much attention and given weightage to the following two characteristics.

1. It is very important for the candidate to establish eye contact directly with whoever is questioning him. This is a sign of confidence and lack of nervousness. Very often the candidate is apt to look away from the interviewer to, look down at his hands; to gaze at the wall, out of the window, etc.. All these attributes are negative points as far as I am concerned. The candidate who looks squarely at the interviewer and answers his questions with a light smile and with confidence is the one that we go for. Of course the content of the answers also matter, but the way in which these are delivered probably get more weightage!!
2. In a group interview, I always look at the attitudes of those who are not speaking at that moment of time. The candidates usually feel that if they are not the ones who are being questioned at a given moment of time, they can relax as the attention has been diverted away from them. This is not so. I find it particularly interesting to watch the

behaviour of those who are not talking and observing the attitudes of the ones who think they are not being studied at that time. Any sign of disinterest or putting up an unacceptable posture goes against that particular candidate. Very often it does happen that a candidate, when he is being directly interviewed, puts up a very good show, but as soon as attention is diverted away from him or her, he lets down his/her guard and through his/her gestures, thus disqualifies himself/herself.

The best thing to do would be to maintain an "interested and keen" look at whoever is being questioned at any given moment of time and also clearly give the impression that he/she is interested in whatever is being discussed, irrespective of the fact that he/she is not participating in the conversation.

By B H Kothari

Chairman, H C Kothari Group of Companies,

Chennai

"I am not sure if the following real life experience was positive or negative, but it was certainly amusing and definitely educative."

In the process of recruiting a Senior Manager for International Trading in Commodities, there have been several interesting cases, but the most interesting was the one where I encountered a very positive person, extremely facile in communication and with good knowledge of the market scenario.

First impressions were not encouraging. The person's gait and appearance bore no connection to his bald pate. Frankly he was hardly the "international image fitting type." I said to myself, "let's ignore the looks, but get on with the fundas." The man certainly knew various buyers and traders who were handling, in this case, agro commodities, all over the world. He also had good knowledge of the domestic supplier base. Last but not the least, he had performed and executed shipments and was a person with "hands on" experience. Besides, he was willing to work to a business plan with a quantity and value target within a specific time frame.

What was I waiting for? He met all our requirements, except possibly the "looks" part. Here was a person who was commercially savvy, knew customers, had a thorough knowledge of suppliers and most importantly a "hands on" person also with working knowledge of the product, its technical aspects, inspection procedures et al.

I finally fired the routine, question, "why was he looking for a change?" It is said that honesty is the best policy; but this man's honesty certainly took me off guard. He stated in Hinglish, "Saar, getting business of even Rs 40 'karod' in the next 6 months is no problem; re-locating to Chennai is not a problem; working on a fixed package with a target based incentive is also no problem. I am looking for an immediate change before the cops get me as our company's directors, 5 out of 6 are already behind bars, the only one remaining is also likely to go in any time – "all on account of various violations relating to forex, tax evasion, etc.!" "I also want to leave before I am commissioned!"

Indeed he was candid. You guessed right; I did not have the "courage" to hire him. I am still wondering what I learnt from this experience. Perhaps you would like to comment?

By *Habil Khorakiwala*
Chairman
Wockhardt Limited

How to Succeed at Interviews

Personnel selection has always been, and will be, a critical and difficult process in an organisation. In India with the job market being as complex as it is, this becomes even more difficult.

Today, we have many people applying for a particular job, but at the same time we have a shortage of good-trained people. This may sound like a contradiction, but it is true. This type of scenario prevails in practically every field of business.

At an organisation, to select and get a good person, both the interviewee and the interviewer have to be good. It is a case where you are selecting a person, and at the same time the same person is selecting your company. It is like a marriage between a boy and a girl. Both must be compatible with each other right at the beginning, or else it will invariably result in disappointment and problems.

In interviewing people for a job you must interview with a purpose:

1. Make the aspirant or candidate give out his/her best. You must make him or her relax, open up and talk. It will help you check out the person's width and depth of knowledge and experience. Get the person to disclose his/her contributions and how he/she will

contribute on the job. For this, ask relevant questions to draw out his/her assumptions.

Listen more than doing all the talking yourself. Don't be overly dominating, or create conditions where the candidate becomes unnecessarily defensive.

2. Search for potential. Potential that is latent and that you can bring out and mould to your and your organisation's advantage or benefit. Invest in people and reap the benefit. Look into his/her growth in line with your own growth. How do you see this actually happening when the person comes aboard?
3. You are looking for a person to join your company. Make him/her want to join the company. Make him/her feel that it is a good and progressive company that he or she is going to join. Offer a career and not just a job – offer him/her a future. Provide him/her information that shows and proves this.
4. Provide him/her with an outline of what you expect of him or her on the job. Give the candidate a job profile and description if you have one. Make the person see an enormous challenge in the job/career at the company – with necessary remuneration and compensation factors and positive working conditions.

The interviewee, or the candidate on the other hand, to be successful in the interview must make it a point to give out the right attitudinal and behavioural signals, besides the personal qualifications and information put out in his or her resume. These should be:

1. Your desire to join the company and making it a long-term career. That you are not a job hopper.
2. You believe in making specific contributions on the job – visible and measurable contributions. Show past examples of this. And project a mindset for being able to do so in the present and future.
3. In contributing to the growth of the company you expect to grow yourself in terms of job satisfaction, knowledge and money – all three at the same time. This will further help in motivating you to do better on the job.
4. You have a professional goal in life – short-term and long-term. Which you are determined to achieve, and will work hard for it.
5. You will have the company's interests and objectives at heart all the time and work towards the achievement effectively and diligently.

You believe in the fact that within the company's growth lies your own career growth.

6. Most of all you will be humble and respectful in behaviour at the interview. You will show good manners, upbringing and character.

By V G Rajadhyaksha
Ex Chairman, Hindustan Lever
Ex Planning Commission Member, Government of India

The Candidate's Revenge

Merit as a basis of recruitment or promotion is often preached but not always practised. Even less common is a policy, which strictly restricts all such recruitment or promotions to merit with no exceptions. I happened to have worked for a company, which had such a policy. It confined recruitment to management trainees except in some rare cases, when the job called for very specialised knowledge and experience, such as scientific research or information technology or legal expertise. Interviewing and selection of all new entrants, especially management trainees by the company, was thus taken very seriously and besides rigorous screening at operational levels, a trainee was finally interviewed by a Board consisting of 2 full time Directors, the Head of Personnel (often a Director himself) and the operating head of the function to which the candidate, if selected, would be assigned – a team of at least 4 very senior people mostly one level below the CEO.

The same degree or even greater degree of attention was paid to promotion or confirmation after probation. Interviewing people was thus a skill, which managers had to learn within 4 or 5 years of joining the company. By the time a manager became a Director, he had interviewed hundreds of people and himself been rigorously assessed by his seniors. Directors can thus perhaps be pardoned if they feel they have developed a sixth sense in evaluating people, although this sometimes leads them astray.

Some companies, including the company I worked for, experimented with professional psychologists as an aid to selection. Our experience, however, was not very happy. The procedure we used was to let the psychologist sit in during the interviews but not permit him to be present at the post interview discussions till the Selection Board had made up its mind. He was then called in to offer his comments. On most occasions, he agreed with the Board but, on occasions, he would point what he thought were character flaws in the candidate and try to explain his reasons. If the Board itself had some doubts about the candidate then the candidate was rejected. We are still not certain if we did the right thing. One interview, in fact, led to the discontinuance of our psychologist. It happened like this:

We had, after going through the interviewing process, settled on a candidate, who the Board was fully satisfied with and we called in the psychologist for his views. He shocked us by saying that he had discovered that he was a secret drinker and was close to becoming a confirmed alcoholic. All of us said that surely a problem like that, would show on his face, or in his movements or speed of reaction and so on, to which he replied that often it doesn't show till it has reached a late stage. He said he would be quite happy if we got a second opinion from another psychologist. This would have been clearly embarrassing, which of course our adviser knew well, so we reluctantly turned the candidate down. Within a week he got another job, presumably with a company who didn't use such arcane selection methods, made a great success of it and now owns a very successful firm.

Perhaps the most memorable interview in my recollection was when, as the Technical Director, I was chairing a Selection Board consisting of the Marketing Director, the Head of Personnel and the General Managers of two of our largest factories, a formidable panel for a young technical trainee, straight out of college, to face. The Marketing Director was an expatriate, a bright young man who had apparently shown great promise in his previous job in an European company. Perhaps as a result of his earlier experience, this Director seemed to have developed a profound contempt however for all non-marketing people especially those from the technical function and was not very good at disguising it.

Expatriates were often sent to India in senior jobs as a part of their career plan and their assignment, usually 3 years, was often regarded as a "make or break" point in their future.

The interviewing process began in the morning by the seven short-listed candidates taking part in two group discussions held entirely amongst themselves on two topics, one chosen by the Selection Board followed by one chosen by mutual consensus. The Board sat in a ring on the periphery of the room, some distance from the candidates but within earshot, and made themselves as inconspicuous as possible and rarely, if ever, intervened. It was quite remarkable how quickly the candidates forgot that the interviewing Board was listening to them. The discussions were followed by each candidate making a short summary of the discussions after which they were given lunch.

Needless to say that the intelligence, articulateness, behavioural pattern and many other personality characteristics of each of the candidates came through to experienced and attentive listeners and by the time this session ended, the Board had arrived at a fairly clear view on which candidates were likely to make the grade. Then followed individual interviews for all the seven candidates when usually, but not always, these preliminary impressions were confirmed. These were truly in-depth interviews and, for the better candidates, it lasted well over an hour.

On this occasion one of these better candidates was a young Sardarji, just out of college and it so happened that he was the last to be interviewed. As Chairman, I began the interviewing process but all the other members of the Selection Board were free to interact with their questions. All of them did so, except the expatriate. So good were the responses of the candidate that we thought that it had become clear that he was an obvious choice. However, as the interview proceeded I could see an appearance of growing bewilderment and annoyance on the face of the Marketing Director. "How could a technical man," he seemed to be saying to himself "give such sensible answers? There must be something wrong." His "sixth sense" was working overtime.

So, after the rest of us had finished I asked him if he had any question to ask the candidate. He then proceeded to ask off-beat questions something like "have you stopped beating your wife" which again the candidate dealt with in a remarkably sensible and mature way much to our secret amusement and the growing discomfiture of the questioner. He then turned round to me and whispered in my ear "You know, he said, "I am sure he has some hidden weakness." So after another ten minutes of questioning he suddenly asked the candidate "Young man, do you have a sense of humour" trying to catch him off-guard. Promptly however came the reply, "Yes Sir, I think I do." "Well then" his inquisitor said, "tell us a joke," to which with a dead pan face he replied "I will" and proceeded to do so and here is what he said:

"There was once a young man who applied for a job in a reputed company. He was shortlisted for the final selection, which began with group discussions followed by a precis. The young man believed he had fared reasonably well by the time it came to the final interview with a

Board of senior company people. Here again he felt that he had answered satisfactorily all the questions put to him by the Board. However, there was one member of the Board who began asking strange questions and it was apparent to the candidate that this member felt that there was something wrong with him, such as being a secret drinker. So to catch him off-guard he suddenly asked the candidate "What is Vat 69?" and promptly came the answer "The Pope's telephone number, Sir."

At this, the flood of amusement, which had been building up inside the other members of the Board, burst out in roars of laughter in which I must say, to his credit, the expatriate joined. For ten minutes or so we were doubled up with pain. I can't remember ever laughing so much. I just managed to gasp out "You are selected" and waved him out of the room and carried on laughing.

Needless to say he made a very promising start in the company but he was too good for even our company to retain and he resigned after working for us for about three years. As for the expatriate, he didn't get a good assessment and soon left the firm.

By Dr P N Singh
Ex-President, Bombay Management Association
Ex-Vice President-Human Resources, A V Birla Group
HR Consultant

The late Aditya Vikram Birla had an uncanny knack of spotting talent. He was also very acutely aware that the success and fast growth of his business empire largely depended on his group's capacity to attract talented professionals. One day, he called me up and asked me to bring some management graduates to be recruited as management trainees for the group. He wanted to interview them himself.

It was a problem for me. The campus recruitment season was already over. I promised to bring some MBAs from the second-rung management institutes, for interview. With great difficulty I screened around 20 MBAs to be interviewed by him.

Time management was always a problem with him, but he tried his best to keep all his commitments. He found a unique interview mechanism to manage his time better. He had a group interview. Three candidates were called together. After a very brief introduction by each candidate, the candidate was asked a relatively simple question by Mr Birla, "What would you like to be in 10 years time in our Group?"

Replies from candidates were more or less similar; Marketing Manager, Head of Marketing, Marketing Executive, Production Manager; Head of Production, Production Executive, Dy General Manager, etc.

After the interviews were over, Aditya Birla said, "Dr Singh, I did not want production managers and marketing managers. I already have many of them. I wanted to recruit potential Presidents for the Group. I want candidates who will like to become Presidents, and not Production Managers in 10 years." He rejected all the candidates.

From Mr Aditya Birla, I learnt three lessons: First, before organising an interview, it should be very clear whether horses, donkeys or elephants were needed. Second, you cannot purchase horses from donkeys' and elephants' markets. And third, a simple question in conjunction with Mr Birla's intuitive sense was enough to gauge the candidates' achievement motivation, ambition and clarity of thought. These were essential qualities in a prospective CEO.

Mr Birla was in need of horses; and had developed his own mechanism for identifying them.

Annexures

Annexure I

Interviews

What Interviewers Should Do and Interviewees Should Know

- Interviewers are expected to avoid questions that could give potentially discriminatory answers (race, religion, national origin, age, sex, handicap, marital status), especially in the USA.
- Interviewers should encourage candidates to talk by asking open ended questions (who, what, when, where, how).
- Interviewers should pay special attention to the non-verbal behaviour of the candidate - i.e. eye contact, gestures, the way the candidate sits, etc.
- Interviewers should be attentive to voice quality, i.e. tone, inflection, emphasis, pauses, speed of speech.
- Interviewers should ask if the information given could be checked by reference checks or by any other means.
- Interviewers want to assess if the applicant comes prepared with knowledge about the Company and its products.
- Interviewers must remember that when asking for Educational Qualifications, it is good to remember that some assignments do not require a college degree.
- Interviewers must ensure that they speak just 30% of the time and listen the rest of the time.
- Interviewers must remember that they need to sell the assignment; as much as the candidate needs to sell himself.

Annexure 2

Permissible Inquiries And Prohibited Inquiries In The United States

Permissible Inquiries

- Appearance as related to job functions
- Authorisation to work in United States
- Education
- Military work experience
- Past job experience

Prohibited Inquiries

- Age
- Colour
- Marital status
- National origin
- Physical/mental disability
- Race
- Religion
- Sex
- Arrest record
- Childcare problems
- Contraceptive practices
- Credit references
- Height and weight
- Plans to have children
- Transportation
- Type of discharge from service
- Unwed motherhood

Annexure 3

Interviewing Outline For A Sales Position

1. Establish Rapport
   - Greetings and introductions
   - Brief chit chat – but avoid religion and politics Weather is a safe subject
2. Set the stage
   - Why? – The purpose of the interview
   - What? – What is the profile of the job/candidate
   - When? – How much time will be taken (we should finish in about an hour!)
3. The Interview
   - Probe using open ended questions
   - listen 60-70% of the time

Can He Do The Job?

A. *Discuss educational experience*
   - Grades
   - Best and worse courses
   - Extracurricular activities (which will indicate leadership and team working qualities).

B. *Discuss work experience*

Begin with earliest jobs and proceed to most recent position.

Briefly discuss:

- Duties and responsibilities
- Expertise
- Significant contributions made
- Likes and dislikes
- Problem Solving
- Reason for leaving (probe deeply for data) for each job.

NOTE: Most of this educational and work information will be on the application. Do not have the applicant repeat what is already given in the resume, except for a few points as a recheck on veracity.

Will He Do The Job?

4. Discuss and evaluate key selection criteria
   - ❍ Customer service orientation
   - ❍ Honesty and integrity
   - ❍ Learning potential
   - ❍ Working under pressure
   - ❍ Team approach
   - ❍ Leadership traits
   - ❍ Detail oriented
   - ❍ Reliability and dependability
5. Inform and sell
   - ❍ company vision, mission, goals
   - ❍ company performance
   - ❍ Ask applicant if he has any questions or comments

Make A Friend – Even If He Doesn't Get The Job

6. Close interview
   - ❍ Tell applicant of next step – the recruiter will be in contact within a certain time frame.
   - ❍ Thank the applicant for his time; and it was a pleasure to make his acquaintance.

(Similar Interview Outlines can be developed for other positions)

Annexure 4

Guidelines For Questions For A Sales Position

I. Work Experience

Factors to Consider

- Is the information you've obtained based on the objective observations that can be verified?
- Is the information consistent with the CV and/or the application?
- Did each new job logically build upon the previous work assignment leading to increased responsibility? Is there a pattern of progress?
- Did the applicant have positive relationships with previous supervisors and customers?

Suggested Questions

1. Tell me about your previous sales experience.
2. With each job, what did you like most? Least?
3. What has contributed most to your career so far?
4. What setbacks or disappointments have you had in your career so far?

II. Administrative Ability

Factors to Consider

- Did it appear that the candidate had done some background work on your Company?
- Was the candidate punctual?
- How has the applicant organised the coverage of his present market?
- Was the candidate prepared with questions?
- Tolerance for paperwork

Suggested Questions

1. Organising/Time Management
    - How do you set up your week or month?
    - How many prospects are available now (in your territory?) How many can you cover weekly, monthly, annually?

- If you were given a sales assignment with X number accounts, what would you do?
- How/when do you set aside time for writing reports? How much time do you set aside for your family? When?

2. Planning
   - How do you organise your sales day in your current job or your last job?
   - How do you plan for a sales call?
   - What do you plan for an emergency – e.g. tender submission?

III. Sales Qualities

Suggested Questions

1. Competitiveness/need for recognition.
   - What was your ranking/performance in your previous position(s)?
   - Do you have sales bulletins where you are mentioned; or letters of commendation?
   - Tell me about your outside activities.
2. Innovation
   - Tell me about 2 situations where you have made a difficult sale.
3. Energy level
   - Describe a normal workday.
   - How many calls do you make in a day?
   - How do you spend your free time? (recheck on 1)
4. Goal Orientation/desire to excel
   - What goals have you set for yourself and met?
   - Did applicant talk about taking charge? About being No1?
   - How do you measure your success and your growth?
5. Initiative /Self-starter
   - What are your outside interests?
   - How did you get this interview?
   - What suggestions for improvement, have you made to your Company?
6. Self-Discipline/Self-Worth
   - How well do you work with others?

- How effectively do you work on your own?
- Have you studied and worked at the same time? Explain.
- Have you ever owned your own business? Explain.
- How well does the candidate deal with disappointment?

7. Money Motivation
   - What have your earnings been? Give gross salary earnings for past 4 years.
   - How have earnings been made up? (base/commission/bonus)
   - Is applicant money motivated? *Mainly/Partly/Not at all*
8. Achievement Motivation
   - What was your greatest contribution in the last 3 years?
   - What was the second?
   - Why do you consider these as great challenges?
9. Communication/Persuasiveness
   - What were the candidate's non verbals like? Did he/she lean forward?
   - Did applicant participate by asking questions, asking for feedback, elaborate on answers?
   - Is applicant persuasive?
   - Is he/she hard to hear?
   - Is candidate assertive?
   - Are general communication skills effective?
10. Ethical Standards
    - Do you think it is wrong to save on allowances, if it does not affect work?
    - If you were to get a higher paid job, a month after joining us, would it be right to resign?
    - If you needed to pay a bribe on the instruction of your boss, what will you do?
    - What are the new product launch plans of your present company?

IV. Other Factors

Suggested Questions

1. Positive or Negative?
   - Anything positive/negative regarding your previous employers?
   - How do you handle difficult people – colleagues or bosses?
   - How do you cope with last minute changes in your assignment?
2. Willingness to Accept Responsibility
   - How much responsibility do you have now? Is it enough?
   - How much responsibility can you handle?
3. Management Potential
   - Have you ever managed people?
   - What are the management characteristics of a boss that you thought were effective? Ineffective?
   - Tell me about your best/worst boss.

(Similar guidelines for questions can be developed for other positions)

Annexure 5

Interview Evaluation Report

Position: Sales Executive

Applicant's Name Date

Please Evaluate The Following Criteria for This Applicant

	Below Average	Average	Good	Excellent
I. Work Experience * comparable experience, * level of responsibility, * past achievements * handling relationships, * past failures	☐	☐	☐	☐
II. **Administrative Ability** * preparation/planning * time management * reporting systems	☐	☐	☐	☐
III. **Sales Qualities**				
1. Goal orientation	☐	☐	☐	☐
2. Initiative	☐	☐	☐	☐
3. Innovativeness	☐	☐	☐	☐
4. Energy level	☐	☐	☐	☐
5. Self-Discipline	☐	☐	☐	☐
6. Competitiveness	☐	☐	☐	☐
7. Money Motivation	☐	☐	☐	☐
8. Achievement Motivation	☐	☐	☐	☐
9. Communication/ Persuasiveness	☐	☐	☐	☐
10. Ethical Standards	☐	☐	☐	☐

IV. Other Factors

* Positive Attitude
* Accepting Responsibility
* Management Potential

	COMMENTS:		RECOMMEND
• Hobbies • Other Interests • Community work		☐ ☐ ☐	HIRE NOT TO HIRE MORE INFORMATION REQUIRED

Name :

Designation :

A = Excellent

B = Good

C = Fair

D = V Poor

(return this page only to personnel upon completion)

Annexure 6

Manager Selection – Evaluation Form

Position : Administrative Manager

Candidate: ____________________

Success Characteristics	Below Average	Average	Good	Excellent
Achievement				
Conceptual Skills				
Creating a Business Vision				
Sharing a Vision				
Communication Skills				
Technical Skills				
Job Knowledge				
Learning Orientation				
Logical Thinking				
Building Corporate Human Skills				
Respect for People/Colleagues				
Judge of People				
Motivation Skills				
Nurturing principles				
High performance Standards				
Setting personal example				

Developing
Team Spirit

Ethical Standards

Change Management

Innovative

Decisive

Entrepreneurial/
Risk Taker

Beyond Work

Family/Stability/
Relationships

Hobbies

Community work

COMMENTS :

RECOMMEND :
- ☐ HIRE
- ☐ NOT TO HIRE
- ☐ MORE INFORMATION REQUIRED

Annexure 7

Sample Offer Letter

March 2 2008

Mr Samir Mark
505, 12th Road
Chembur
Mumbai 400 071

Dear Samir

It is a pleasure to write to you and welcome you to the Marketing Advisory Services Group! I look forward to working with you in your new role as Associate Consultant of the MAS Group.

Samir, the following will summarise our employment offer and your subsequent acceptance:

1. Annual consolidated salary of Rs 6,00,000 beginning 1 April 2008. Your first salary review will be on 1 April 2009.
2. Your participation in MAS Group's bonus plan will be based on 25% of your annual salary. This plan is based on company achievement of 15% growth above prior year's profit; and a minimum specified contribution from clients in your portfolio.
3. The MAS Group will pay for moving your family and household possessions from Bangalore to Mumbai at actuals, up to a maximum of Rs 15,000/-.
4. Annual vacation will be 30 working days per annum.

Please sign a copy of this letter and return it to me as a token of your agreement. I am delighted that you will now be part of the MAS Group.

Yours sincerely

Signed and agreed to:

Walter Vieira
President
MAS Group
Enclosure:

Samir Mark

Annexure 8

Sample Regret Letter

March 2 2008

Mr Samir Roy
505, 12th Road
Chembur
Mumbai 400 071

Dear Mr Roy

Let me first apologise for the time of six weeks that it took us to arrive at a decision. I recall I had told you that we would let you know the results within four weeks.

We had a difficult time taking a final decision. The race was very closely run. It was a question of a head length that made the difference. Although you came very close, we had to decide on another candidate who had a slightly more appropriate background to fit the requirements of the assignment. Our regret is in no way a reflection of your professional experience and qualifications. The panel of interviewers was in fact, very impressed with the progress you have made in the short period of just five working years.

We wish you all the very best in your future career, and thank you for applying to the MAS Group.

With kind regards, and once again, our best wishes.

Yours sincerely

Walter Vieira